YOUR
Marriage

Michael and Myrtle Baughen

EDITOR: JOHN STOTT

Hodder & Stoughton
LONDON SYDNEY AUCKLAND

Designed and created by
Three's Company
12 Flitcroft Street
London WC2H 8DJ.

Worldwide co-edition organised and
produced by Angus Hudson Ltd,
Concorde House, Grenville Place,
Mill Hill, London NW7 3SA.
Tel +44 81 959 3668
Fax +44 81 959 3678

Picture acknowledgments
Ebenezer Pictures: pp. 7, 9, 17, 25, 31,
41, 59, 62, 71, 75, 79, 95, 101, 127,
135
Tiger Design: p. 35
Zefa: front cover, pp. 47, 83, 87

British Library Cataloguing in
Publication Data
A catalogue record for this book is
available from the British Library.

ISBN 0 340 60023 3 (casebound)
ISBN 0 340 61255 X (paperback)

Typeset by Watermark, Cromer.
Printed in Singapore.

Hodder and Stoughton Ltd
A Division of Hodder Headline PLC
338 Euston Road
London NW1 3BH

Contents

Questions for discussion are set out at the end of each chapter. It would be very easy to read this book and even to agree with it but not to let the truths it teaches challenge and affect the marriage you are contemplating or perhaps are already in. The questions are designed to help you review what you have read and then apply what you learn to your situation. They are intended for you to discuss as a couple, although you might find it helpful to put your ideas on paper individually first and then compare notes together.

Andrew and Rachel Baughen

Foreword

Before Michael Baughen became Bishop of Chester, while he was still Rector of All Souls, Langham Place, I was the Baughens' near neighbour. So I had ample opportunity to observe their married and family life, and I can testify to the integrity of what they write here.

The joint authorship of a book often does not work. But in this case it does, because Michael and Myrtle know and understand one another so well.

Your Marriage avoids the opposite extremes of cynicism and romanticism. It is a rich blend of Christian faithfulness, wisdom, common sense, honesty, candour and humour. And the whole text is written in an engaging style of 'from us to you' directness.

Couples contemplating marriage, or preparing for it, will find here the fruits of long experience and reflection. Special readings from the Bible and prayers are provided for use before, during and after the honeymoon.

Clergy will find in *Your Marriage* an ideal book to give to couples they are seeking to prepare for their wedding day. And the questions at the end of each chapter make the book a useful guide for discussion groups.

It was Jesus himself who described a married couple as 'joined together by God'. I am confident that readers of this book will gain a clearer understanding of God's unchanging purpose for married life.

John Stott

Introduction

This is a book for couples approaching marriage although much of it could be a means of check-up for couples already married. It springs out of our experience both as a married couple and in preparing other couples for marriage, and from what we have been taught by contemporary young married couples. We are also grateful for the valuable comments of our daughter and sons, and their spouses, on the earlier drafts of the book; these produced numerous emendations.

The book is not a 'marriage troubleshooter' but it does aim to suggest ways of thinking that can avoid trouble, or identify its causes should trouble occur.

We are conscious of many failings in our partnership but we are also more thankful for each other than we can say – and thankful to God for the joy and privilege of marriage and family life over the last thirty-six years.

If you have your hearts firmly rooted in the limitless love of God, with a realistic awareness of the reality of sin in your nature and of the power of God's grace, and an overwhelming love for one another, you are heading towards marriage at its best – God's best.

May God's blessing be on you richly now and always.

Michael and Myrtle Baughen
Spring 1992

1. Christian Marriage is Wonderful!

Marriage is great; Christian marriage is wonderful!

Her Majesty Queen Elizabeth II put it succinctly in her speech on the occasion of her Silver Wedding: 'A few well-chosen words can often say more than volumes. When the Bishop was asked what he thought about sin, he replied with simple conviction that he was "against it". If I am asked today what I think about family life after twenty-five years of marriage I can answer with equal simplicity and conviction, "I am for it."' So are we!

Of course, however much you feel you love each other at this present moment, your love has to mature and maturity comes in the problems as well as in the joys. Your whole relationship can be a constantly growing, deepening and even healing experience. This is a central part of the privilege and richness of a marriage united in love.

Many voices speak out today against marriage. They are heard frequently in television programmes, films, plays, books and magazines. They argue that institutionalised sexual and family relations are not ordained by God or even by nature. Yet the alternative, of men and women living together without a lifelong commitment, is only a pale shadow of the reality of a loving marriage.

God's plan
Nobody will ever find a better pattern for human relationship than marriage because it is ordained by God and he, as the Creator, knows what is best for human beings. That marriage can often be warped by sin is painfully obvious, but this does not alter the basic truth that marriage is the intended and, therefore, the best pattern. In the face of all the denigrating attacks on marriage we, like so many others, want to shout from the housetops that marriage can be great and that Christian marriage can be wonderful. The objec-

Marriage is great; Christian marriage is wonderful!

tors may have the voice of the media but the rest of us need to be heard too!

So put the smear campaign against marriage out of your mind. Do not let it influence your thinking. Instead, realise that what lies ahead for you is the very best for you both. You will have fun and sadness, laughter and tears, successes and failures, but together you will find a deepening joy throughout your married life. There is much to help you and guide you – no marriage can survive without both partners working at it. But if you belong to Christ, then you have him with you and in you by his Spirit, and he is the greatest helper of all.

The teaching of Genesis 1

God's plan for marriage was there from the beginning. Look at Genesis chapters 1 and 2. In 1:27 we are told that human beings are the climax of creation. They are marked out in a unique way from all animal life because they are made 'in the image of God', with all the special divine facets of creativity, true love, intelligent relationships and worship. 'Male and female he created them,' and they are to 'be fruitful and increase in number' (1:28). All this is 'very good' (1:31).

The teaching of Genesis 2

In Genesis 2, where there is a complementary approach to the theme, we are told, 'It is not good for the man to be alone' (verse 18). Verses 18–24 lead us straight to marriage, laying the foundation of physical differences, the procreation of the continuing human race and the relationship of companionship. This is sealed in 2:24: 'For this reason a man will leave his father and mother and be united to his wife, and they will become one flesh.' There is no suggestion here or at any point in Scripture that any other pattern is intended by the creator in his perfect will for men and women. This is a creation principle and thus stands for all time.

New Testament teaching

When our Lord speaks about marriage he quotes Genesis 2:24 and adds: 'Therefore what God has joined together, let man not separate' (Mark 10:6–9). There was no concept of marriage as a lifeboat packed with divorce and separation lifebelts. Although the possibility of divorce or separation may have to be faced, it has to be the very last resort, for our Lord's intention is that we marry for life and mature with the difficulties as well as the successes. So, be clear from the start that a lifelong commitment *is* the creator's intention and that with Christ in our marriage we can experience an even richer fulfilment of God's creation purpose for us.

It is also our Lord's design that sexual intercourse should only take place within marriage. If it takes place outside marriage it is an abuse of God's plan and will. It should be an act of total self-giving as the climax of the marriage relationship. We are more than animals. We are human beings made in the image of God, and therefore made for a deep personal relationship.

Society in first-century Corinth was in an appalling moral quagmire. In 1 Corinthians 6, Paul describes it as a place of the 'immoral, idolaters, adulterers, sexual perverts, thieves, the greedy, drunkards, revilers, and robbers'. Sounds modern enough, doesn't it? Then he says: 'And such were some of you. But you were washed, you were sanctified, you were justified in the name of the Lord Jesus Christ and in the Spirit of our God' (1 Corinthians 6:9–11, RSV). That was the gospel's transforming power – just as it is today. Christ can restore a true view of relationships of every kind, including the sexual.

Christian marriage

Is there such a thing as 'Christian marriage'? Should we expect marriage between Christians to be distinctive? Those who do not think there can be 'Christian marriage' base their opinion on the creation narrative. They argue that all marriages – whether Christian or not – are created by God. Of course, that is true, but when we are in Christ we are in a wonderful new dimension that lifts marriage and alters it into a triangular relationship of each partner to the other and to Christ.

The headship, or Lordship, of Christ is what makes a Christian marriage. This is the thrust of that marvellous passage in Ephesians 5:21–33 (see page 140) where the creation foundation of marriage is raised to sublime heights of love in Christ. The marriage partnership is centred on subjection to one another '*out of reverence for Christ*' (Ephesians 5:21). The couple are part of Christ's Church – his body. He is the head of the Church, the one who cherishes and nourishes it and has such splendid intentions for it, and thus for its members. The pervading and distinguishing mark of Christian marriage is Christ, with his purposes and love over all and in all.

In 1 Peter 3:7 Paul tells husbands to 'live with your wives . . . as heirs with you of the gracious gift of life'. We both have access to his grace, individually and together, and can draw on those inexhaustible riches to assist us, guide us and bring us into maturity in our marriage. It is said that two's company and three's none but when the third person is Christ it is wonderful. This Christ-centredness is something to which we will return later, but it is the crucial difference, the distinguishing mark of Christian marriage.

Marriage with a difference

As Christians we also have a different attitude to the use of time, talents and possessions, as well as to purpose and values, to aims and priorities. Our faith affects our attitudes to our children – the value we place on their lives and individual development, the way we pray for and with them, and our worship together. It also affects the use of the home and our attitudes to our neighbours.

We shall think this through more fully and practically in the pages to come, but we need to say it here to underline the differences in Christian marriage.

The sexual relationship is also heightened in Christian marriage. Far from thinking of sex as 'dirty' or somehow sub-Christian, Christians should have the highest view of it. The warping and twisting of the sex theme in the media day after day can tarnish our thinking. We have to try and cleanse ourselves from that and see the sexual relationship in marriage as God-intended and beautiful. Sexual desire is part of our being and thus is God-created.

Erotic beauty is richly expressed in the Song of Solomon in the Old Testament. Some have spiritualised this book and turned it into an allegory of our relationship with Christ, expounding it in terms of a deeply spiritual love-relationship with him. There certainly is much in the book that can inspire and enrich that relationship. Yet, as we shall see in chapter 7, it is primarily a lovers' book and uses the intimate language of sexual love. The sexual relationship needs advice and understanding – and, again, we shall return to this theme in chapter 7 – but in the context of deep love, and especially when that love is inspired, enriched and deepened by the love of Christ, it is glorious, beautiful and sublime. How often we thank our Lord for love in our marriage relationship, not least in the sexual expression of it. All this is the plan and intention of the creator for human beings; but without Christ it can so often be ruined or marred, whereas with Christ it can be fulfilled and grow towards perfection.

Looking forward
So take hold of the fact that as you approach marriage you are coming to a great and wonderful state of life, planned and intended by God. Pause together and in a deliberate moment thank God for his institution of marriage and for the prospect of sharing your life together.

Then, if you are Christians, realise how your marriage will have so much more going for it. You have Christ now. As you love him together and know his love, he will raise your thoughts and attitudes above the murky waters of non-Christian thinking into his attitudes, his values, his purposes and his best for marriage.

We do so hope that you will find marriage to be far more than you even dream it to be at this time. Cynics say it starts sweet and goes sour. Others say that the romantic expectations of marriage are quickly dashed. That may be so for many, sadly. It has not been so for us and it need not be for you. Approach marriage as members of Christ, but also with the Christian realism that you are still sinners with inbred selfishness. Christians are to be both idealists and yet realists about what we are and need to become. We are to be realistic romantics!

Then, believe us, it gets better all the way. Love grows – we are more in love now than ever – and we thank God for all that it has meant to us both to be married in Christ. With all our heart we say: Marriage is great; Christian marriage is wonderful!

Questions for discussion

Having read in this first chapter that marriage is good, and that Christian marriage is even better, consider the following questions:

1. What is your view of marriage? Reflect on couples you know (maybe your parents or contemporaries) and their marriages. What aspects of their relationship do you like or dislike? Can you learn from their experience?
2. From reading this introductory chapter, review together the key components of a Christian marriage. How is it different from a marriage between those who do not hold to Christian beliefs?
3. As you contemplate marriage, is your view of the future a Christian one? Where do you stand before God? Will your marriage be one where Christ is the head?

2. Are You in Love?

'Will you love her/him. . . ?' This is the key wedding question and, although it may seem superfluous if you feel madly in love with each other, it is vital to realise that love will have to rest on more than feelings if it is to be genuine, lasting, and deepening. Love is also unlikely to last if you are hesitant and doubtful about it before the wedding.

A question of meaning
'Love' must be the most misused word in the English vocabulary, occurring in the majority of pop songs and given as the reason for all manner of sexual and non-sexual activities and aberrations. It has become totally detached from rules, laws or guidelines – it floats free.

Thus, some would say that if you can call a thought or action 'love' then it is all right. If the Bible disagrees, then dispense with the Bible; if society disagrees, then change society. 'All you need is love. . .' is the popular slogan for this devalued and diffuse meaning of love. So for many people sexual intimacy is justified, and moral rules may be discounted, as long as love is felt. The confusion that has resulted has been colossal. Little wonder that some anti-marriage campaigners are saying that 'love is a word screaming for redefinition'.

In our home we had a boiler that was difficult to handle. Our instruction leaflet was for a different type of boiler, although one made by the same company. Eventually, after much frustration, we wrote to the manufacturer to ask for the correct instruction leaflet. When it arrived it became easy to handle the boiler. We needed the maker's original instructions. Similarly, in the current confusion over the meaning of 'love' the Maker's definitions and instructions are what we all need to hear and follow; these make sense, enabling us to love – to the full.

Person to person

'God is love.' Those words from 1 John 4:16 start many wedding services. Love is not so much feelings, attitudes or actions – it is primarily a Person. Love is about the relationships of persons. Time and again, throughout the Bible, God establishes covenants with his people – and his covenants are almost always love-covenants. We read of a covenant being made, for instance, between God and Abraham, and of another after the giving of the Ten Commandments through Moses.

The tragedy of Old Testament history is that so often the people failed to keep their side of the covenant agreement. This not only resulted in judgement but it brought pain to the heart of God. The pain was not over the breaking of the letter of the agreement, it was over the breaking of the relationship. Love is person to person. A contract such as that in a wedding is only a form of words; its reality is in the heart. It is this which makes adultery so devastating. Whilst it certainly breaks the 'contract', adultery, in its yielding to a person other than the marriage partner, is essentially an offence against the person.

This is vividly demonstrated in the book of Hosea. Here the prophet sees the unfaithfulness of his wife as a parable of Israel's unfaithfulness to God. It is not that Israel has stopped its worship activities – its services and offering of sacrifices – but that it has stopped its heart-love, and so the relationship is broken. The climax comes in Hosea 6:6: 'I desire steadfast love and not sacrifice, the knowledge of God, rather than burnt offerings' (RSV).

In the same way, New Testament Christians can slip out of the love-centred relationship to God and rely instead on activities and achievements. So in the most famous chapter about love – 1 Corinthians 13 – Paul writes:

If I speak in the tongues of men and of angels, but have not love, I am a noisy gong or a clanging cymbal. And if I have prophetic powers and understand all mysteries and all knowledge, and if I have all faith, so as to remove mountains, but have not love, I am nothing. If I give away all I have, and if I deliver my body to be burned, but have not love, I gain nothing. (verses 1–3, RSV)

Notice Paul's words: 'I am nothing . . . I gain nothing.' The futility of trying to maintain a relationship without love comes because love is the heart of true relationship.

We can see how this applies to marriage and we might adapt Paul's words to say: 'If we speak love-words, express love-intentions and exercise love-acts, yet do not have love, we are living a falsity; if we help one another in the home, remember anniversaries, send flowers or make phone calls when we are away, yet do not have love, we are shamming.' So it is vital that we are truly in love! That means *now*, before the wedding, and increasingly over the years – for, obviously, love has to grow.

Self-giving love
Several aspects of love are involved in a full understanding of love as God meant it to be. We shall look at friendship love, sexual love and family love later in the book, but here in this chapter we want to concentrate on the highest expression of love, the love that is highlighted above all others in the New Testament. This is *agape* – self-giving love. *Agape* is the Greek word used in the New Testament to describe God's love for his people, and it is the word used most of all throughout the New Testament to refer to the sort of love God's people should show to God and to one another. It is *the* word for you to ponder, and think through in its practical outworking, now before the wedding and then throughout your married life. It directly confronts those who say that marriage is merely a way of controlling others, or a means of satisfying one's own ego and security needs. These people see partners as a kind of very elaborate furniture in each other's lives. Strident voices in many media presentations and magazine articles about marriage and the family stress the underlying notion that marriage is for one's own self-fulfilment. No! says God. It is the precise opposite. Self-giving love wants the fulfilment of one's spouse. This transforms attitudes and enables love to grow, deepen and become increasingly wonderful.

A pattern for marriage
It is this 'self-giving' word which is used in that superb passage of Scripture referring to marriage – Ephesians 5:22–33 (see page 140). The first words of chapter 5 give the reason for loving in this

Love must rest on more than feelings if it is to be genuine.

way – because we are to 'imitate God': 'Be imitators of God, therefore, as dearly loved children and live a life of love. . .' We are his 'dearly loved' children and so we will want most of all to be like him. This means living with self-giving love in every aspect of our lives, '. . . just as Christ loved us and gave himself up for us as a fragrant offering and sacrifice to God' (Ephesians 5:2).

This is the standard. The more we live like this in *all* relationships, the more lovely and wholesome life becomes for everyone, including ourselves.

Paul next condemns all that is offensive to such self-giving love – sexual immorality, impurity, greed, obscenity and the like – before he returns to highlight more clearly this theme of self-giving love as it applies in marriage. On the way he reminds us of our need to be constantly filled with the Holy Spirit and to be always giving thanks to God – both very necessary antidotes to the subversive influences of the world around us.

'Submit to one another out of reverence for Christ,' Paul instructs at the start of the key paragraph beginning at verse 21.

This is self-giving to the full. You cannot submit without trust and without wanting the best fulfilment for the other. Paul's words directly oppose any form of manipulation for your own ends. Only by seeing this sentence as fundamental to the paragraph can we understand the meaning of the following words, 'Wives, submit to your husbands. . . For the husband is the head of the wife. . .' This is not a mandate for bossiness, for power or domination, but for serving, care and the smooth running of the relationship.

The instruction to let the husband be the head is matched by many verses spelling out his responsibility to his wife in sacrifice, service, working for her well-being and desiring the very best for her. These days there is often a reaction against the idea of head-ship, but this is probably because the concept has become abused. There are some interesting interpretations, of course. Charles Haddon Spurgeon told the bride at the first wedding service he conducted: 'Don't try to be the head but you be the neck, then you can turn the head whichever way you like!' Others have suggested that the man is the head and the woman the influence.

What we are really talking about in God's pattern for marriage is a mutual bond of trust and of joint action. Both partners cannot take the titular leadership. There are, of course, marriages where the wife seems to take the lead and this can work. But perhaps man is bidden to take this role because of greater physical strength – it is certainly not because of greater intelligence or value! Or perhaps it is the innate shyness of the male species that needs to be helped by the role of headship. But whatever the reasons, the most perfect love-marriages certainly seem to be ones in which there is a quiet, loving, gentle and effective acceptance by both of headship respon-sibilities for the man, matched by his total self-giving, and the wife's total self-giving and her constructive partnership in leader-ship.

A change of attitude

In the outworking of this pattern given to us by God it is the qual-ity of the man's self-giving that is often open to question. He may be inclined to take the headship without a genuine acceptance of the servant role. As a single man he may well have been making decisions and leading others and may expect to continue doing so. In marriage he has to change. The marriage relationship is not the sort of relationship in which only one person makes the decisions. The woman may also have been in a responsible leadership role, and will bring much, if not more, expertise to the marriage. So now decision-making must be shared, with much discussion about what to do, how to act, what to buy and so on.

The man also has to learn (and it seems a long process) what it means to work for the best for his wife – for her joy and fulfilment as a person. An enormous amount of understanding needs to come from him if, for instance, the wife has given up her career and is 'stuck at home' with three children under the age of five. The need for her to find some other fulfilment is discussed later (chapter 8) but here we want to point out that the husband should be ahead of his wife in making suggestions, and active in enabling them to become realities.

A question of value
Do you value one another as equal in the sight of God? The Trinity has within it different roles, but all the members of the Trinity are one – equal in substance and love. Husband and wife are one in flesh and, as Christians, one in Christ. In Ephesians 5:28–9 Paul tells husbands to 'love their wives as their own bodies. He who loves his wife loves himself. After all, no one ever hated his own body, but he feeds and cares for it. . .' Somewhere deep down in some people is the false idea that men are superior to women. It may be that the headship theme has been misinterpreted in that way. In many countries of the world, the subjugation, denigration and inferiority of the status of women are appalling. The New Testament's challenge that there is no longer 'male and female' because we are 'all one in Christ Jesus' (Galatians 3:28) still has a long way to go in transforming society's attitudes.

A husband must reject all non-Christian attitudes – and they usually lurk more strongly than we realise. One of the greatest complaints from wives is that they are devalued. That simply must not be, and if devaluing occurs in any form we must as marriage partners face it and challenge it. Men – your wife's value, worth and being – all that she is – are equal to yours. Ephesians 5 is God's instruction to value your wife as you value yourself – no lesser standard is permitted. As Charles Haddon Spurgeon put it, a model marriage is 'founded on pure love and cemented in mutual esteem'.

Love in action

So much for the principle and the pattern, but what about the practicalities? Romantic ideals of love seem rather different at 7 o'clock on a cold winter's morning when the baby is crying, the toast burns and the car will not start! You will often need to remind yourselves of the principles if you are to keep your marriage on the right love-navigation course.

However, there is plenty of practical wisdom about love and relationship in the New Testament. The most famous is in 1 Corinthians chapter 13 (see page 140). We have already mentioned the opening verses, so look now at verse 4. Here is a surprise. In verses 4, 5 and 6 there are only two positive statements about love: 'Love is patient and kind.' This seems somewhat less than romantic – at first sight almost patronising or a putting-up with each other. But, of course, it is much more positive than that! Patience is a very strong attribute. It springs out of acceptance and respect; it curbs instant reaction because it thinks more deeply about why something has happened and sees a fuller perspective; it believes in the possibility of change over a period of time; it wants the best and meanwhile accepts the present reality. Patience also realises that an angry reaction may be primarily the result of one's own state of health or mind, rather than someone else's fault.

In the same way, kindness is a positive heart response rising out of a deep care for the other person and a willingness to put oneself to trouble and effort. Whenever the response of one's partner is, in word or attitude, 'How kind,' you are on target. In other words, however much you may *say* you love someone, you will really prove it by your patient refusal to react with irritation or anger and by your thinking and acting with understanding and caring sensitivity.

It is now that Paul lists the negatives. You might not have expected this list in a chapter describing love, but a little thought soon shows its effectiveness. After all, Paul has just given the major tests of love: Is there evidence of real self-giving between you and do you relate to each other with patience and kindness (even when the other is consistently late or untidy or forgets the tickets . . .)?

Now here are some further tests:

- Are you or is your partner jealous or boastful? There is, of course, a right jealousy aimed at safeguarding the exclusiveness of your relationship together, but the jealousy and boastfulness referred to here are marks of an ego trip, perhaps caused by insecurity, and are not love.

- Are you or is your partner arrogant or rude, perhaps not to one another, but to others? If it is happening to others now it is an indication that the self is being put first, and this raises queries about whether there is a spirit of love. In a marriage this attitude is disastrous.

- Are you or is your partner always insisting on your own way? Again, this is a manifestation of self-centredness, an attitude that is very difficult to live with and can rapidly wreck a love-marriage.

- Are you or is your partner irritable or resentful? It would not be very easy to live with this sort of person for the rest of one's life!

- Do you or does your partner rejoice at wrong, or in the right? Hopefully the latter, or there will always be a bias to finding fault and this will be a running sore in your life together.

In verse 7 Paul returns to some positives: 'Love bears all things, believes all things, hopes all things, endures all things.' This sort of love is encouraging, visionary and secure. It is what you both need.

We would like to add a few more 'tests' from what we have observed.

Are you:

- Proud of each other (in the right sense of that term)?
- Able to respect each other?
- Willing to forgive each other?
- Frequently laughing together and getting much joy in being together?
- Secure enough together sometimes to enjoy silence as well as conversation?

Try these questions too:

> • Do you find new strength and purpose when you are together – or the opposite?
> • Can you share spiritual things, and are you growing spiritually because of your friendship?
> • Do you and your partner want to give more than receive?
> • Are there habits, characteristics or personality traits in you or your partner that worry, annoy or irritate either of you? (but remember that people who are 'perfectionist' in all their ideals will never find a partner who is a human being!)
> • Would you and your partner like the other to be the father/mother of your children?

Face the facts

Bill and Lynne Hybels in their helpful book *Fit to be Tied* (published by Zondervan) speak about the difficulties they have had in their partnership and urge those facing marriage to be 'ruthlessly honest' about their motives for marrying. For example, they ask, 'Are you looking for a life preserver? Are you carrying hurts and disappointments that you secretly hope a spouse can heal? Do you have unfinished business with parents or others that you need to resolve before you can build a healthy relationship?' Similarly, they urge: 'You must observe potential mates very carefully: look below the surface. What kind of expectations do potential mates have? What excess baggage are they carrying? What is their agenda?'

All this sounds a bit of a marathon but it is just being realistic. It is all too easy to get carried away or be swept off one's feet, and such 'love' can blind us to potential problems and weaknesses. We certainly believe in a glowing and heart-throbbing love – we fell in love almost at first sight and there seemed little need to test that love, as it rang true on all levels (even though we were and are so imperfect). Yet if there is a sense of unease, a feeling that something is not 'ringing true', you need to stop and test the relationship. This is to be a marriage for life – 'till death us do part'. The basis of the marriage relationship is self-giving love. On your wedding day you will promise to love each other 'as long as you both shall live'. So it is vital to ask the question seriously now: 'Am I in love?'

Questions for discussion

Having considered what constitutes marriage, we now reflect on the subject of love and how this is a crucial foundation of a marriage relationship.

1. Before reading this chapter, how would you have defined love? What examples of love in action can you think of?

2. By way of review, consider what it is that constitutes self-giving love. It might be useful to read through Ephesians 5 again together and then discuss the components of self-giving love.

3. Work through all the questions that come out of 1 Corinthians 13 (set out at the end of the book). Rather than skipping through them, discuss each one, trying to think of examples of when the issues have been relevant.

4. Having worked through this chapter on love, does your relationship stand firm? Do you need to change your view of love?

3. Courtship and Engagement

Courtship is a glorious time of discovery, a time of much fun and freedom. We have so many happy memories of our own courtship, not least of the proposal and acceptance on the down platform of Penge West Railway Station – observed with enjoyment by the man in the signal-box! We laugh together at the memory of our first outing in the countryside, when we were followed and surrounded by swarms of flies as we walked through the woods. We ended up walking together with a raincoat over our heads! You will probably never again be as free as you are now. So set out to enjoy your courtship to the full.

Friendship
Your key to this time of courtship is friendship, one of the four great loves described in C. S. Lewis' book *The Four Loves*. (The other three are affection, Eros (erotic love) and *agape* love, that is, charity.) You need to put friendship at the top of your courtship agenda. This may seem a little strange in view of all we have just written about the pre-eminence of *agape* love, but there is no contradiction. Rather, friendship runs parallel to *agape* love and in many senses is an expression of it. We will be seeing later in the chapter that sexual intercourse before marriage is not God's intention for you and, apart from the religious and moral issues, one reason is that sexual intercourse during courtship and engagement is a diversion from the development of friendship. The physical sexual act is a private matter but friendship is much more public and does not need to be in secret. This is a time for exposing your personalities to each other before you expose your bodies.

Friendship love is far more important than we often realise. For one thing, it is eternal. Sexual love may fade in old age or become impossible through an accident or illness, but friendship is for all

Put friendship at the top of your agenda!

the years of our life and beyond – it is for ever. In heaven, we are not given in marriage, as our Lord explained (Mark 12:25), but we will be united in deep love, especially friendship love. Unless you take this seriously now you will have problems in your marriage.

On many occasions when we have been asked to help with marriage difficulties we have found the cause of the problem to be a failure to develop friendship before marriage. We can think of a missionary couple who met on the mission field. They were both delightful people and, while fully and demandingly committed to the mission work, they became engaged and were married. They continued together in the same work, and this was all right until they returned to England, to a very different situation. It was then, with the strong rhythm and demands of mission work removed, that they found they did not know each other. They had never become friends. Their marriage was deeply marred, and it was a long and painful process to develop that missing part of love's essential relationship.

There can be many reasons why friendship love has not grown. It may be that engagement and marriage have come too quickly, or there has been a sexual relationship almost from the beginning, or the engaged couple have had very little opportunity to spend time together before marriage (if, for example, they have been living and working in places far apart). But whatever the reason, time and time again this failure has resulted in trouble.

Sexual love is a one-to-one relationship, whereas friendship love is essentially two people alongside each other, sharing, exploring and enjoying all sorts of interests and people, and finding their relationship cemented in the process. It is often illustrated like this:

In the process of friendship love the bonds of mutual trust and understanding grow naturally. You do not need to be introspective to see whether or not this is happening, but from time to time you will stop and realise just how much you have grown to know each other.

Sharing interests
Each of you will have come to this partnership with rich experiences of life – its joys as well as its wounds and pains. You may have different skills and talents, different hobbies and sporting interests, different tastes in food, different preferences for television programmes, films and music, and possibly different church affiliations. Of course, you may have identical tastes and abilities – but if so your friendship may not be so stimulating! Normally there are all sorts of differences which can form the agenda for fun and discovery, though this demands sensitivity from the partner who is good at something or who knows the place or subject well.

You will want to introduce your partner to your 'favourite place in the world'. If you can afford it, you will try and go there for a weekend or a holiday – or you will talk about the place if you need to 'save it' for later years. You are a tennis fanatic? Great! One of us is, and one of us is not – and that remains so! However, lack of ability need not mean a lack of support for your partner, and often you may each come thoroughly to enjoy the other's favourite sport or hobby. Both of us now share a love of railways (though not to the same extent!) – but only one of us did at the beginning. Being involved in a sport will, of course, always be more fun than watching it; the fellow on the rugby pitch will enjoy himself more than his fiancée shivering in the stand – and he should not think of going off with his mates for the rest of the evening unless it is 'fellows and girls together'. Sharing must be impregnated with understanding if it is to develop into real friendship.

It is also important to take up interests you can explore together with equal pleasure. This, of course, will apply to interests you already have in common – it may be that you met through those very interests.

However, engagement is a great time to explore new interests and activities which you can enjoy learning and discovering together. For instance, have you both always meant to learn the guitar? Tackle it together. Are there any domestic skills you *need* to learn in preparation for setting up a home? How is your cooking, for example, or your handling of basic electrics, your do-it-yourself skills and so on? Why not attend classes together? Or perhaps you have both always meant to climb Snowdon? Do it together. You have never been to an opera? Try for the cheapest seats in the upper circle. You have never been to Paris? If you can afford it, what better place to enjoy during courtship?

The comparative freedom you have during courtship and engagement often enables you to act on the spur of the moment – a lovely Saturday and off you can go to the coast for the day; you are unexpectedly offered seats for a show or film and you can snap them up. The fun of a surprise outing; the opportunity to work together or to help someone, perhaps in an annual spring-clean at church or as you cook lunch for friends; the shopping trips and the enjoyment of commenting on the clothes each is thinking of buying – all are opportunities to grow into friendship. So enjoy becoming friends, enjoy just being together, learning together and doing things together.

Sharing yourselves
This friendship will enable you to share your inner selves. Are

there things that have secretly worried you about life, or about yourself or the prospect of marriage? Have there been other boy-friends or girlfriends and if so, who are they and why did the friendships end? (Either of you may later meet an ex-boy/girlfriend of your partner, and it is better to know about them beforehand!) It may be that you will need to admit to a rash act of sexual inter-course or an affair. As friendship between you becomes more sec-ure you will (and must) be able increasingly to open your hearts to each other.

This openness includes a spiritual dimension. If you are both Christians you are a brother and sister in Christ. As his friends you need to talk about him, sharing your experiences, and uniting more and more deeply in love for him. There may be denomi-national differences to talk through, or different emphases of Christian understanding. Any fears, doubts or hang-ups in spiritual things need to be shared. You will learn to pray together (we first did so when a walk brought us to a village and we went into the church and prayed). Worshipping together, talking over the sermon, sharing in Christian fellowship and in Christian ser-vice will all be vital to a friendship love permeated by the friendship love of Christ. One of the marks of your being right for each other will be a growing sense of spiritual affinity.

Your friends and family

The openness of this growing friendship will mean you can share easily with one another's friends in activities and events. Your mutual friendship will normally mean that you naturally gravitate together in these activities, and give priority to each other. Friends will respect and encourage your friendship together (and will tease you). You must, however, be sensitive. You must beware of giving your unmarried friends unnecessary hurt and you must be careful how you express affection in public. If it emerges that one partner is putting the wishes of other friends first, then you will need to face that together. It is deceptively easy to 'snap back' into an earl-ier relationship with friends. That must not happen. Requests by friends to do what they want will have to be considered by both of you together.

You will also need to visit your family homes, where your friendship will need to be open towards relatives. Yet here again you can all too easily revert back to old ties and priorities, and it is important to remember that your first loyalty is to each other.

Disagreements

It is almost inevitable that you will have differences of opinions and actions and these can cause friction unless you learn to be open with one another. Bill and Lynne Hybels in *Fit to be Tied* warn, 'Why is it that people who are courting describe their potential spouses with phrases like "charming idiosyncrasies" and "delightfully spontaneous" when what they really ought to call them is *irresponsible?*'

This is the result of what psychologists call *blockage*, a term used to describe the tendency to block out reality in the excitement of being in love. So avoid blockage. Be open. 'Wounds from a friend can be trusted,' says Proverbs 27:6, and your friendship with each other should allow for and benefit from your openness in discussion, in listening and in constructive comment. We would be less than honest if we did not say that this is not easy and requires more sensitivity than was ours in our earlier days – so keep at it! Indeed, that applies to friendship love in general. What begins in courtship and engagement needs to go on developing all through your life together.

Remember that our Lord said that the highest mark of friendship is the willingness to lay down your life for your friends (John 15:13). Although you are not likely to be required to do that, its spirit – valuing your friend higher than you value yourself – is of the deepest value in your friendship. If you can get to that way of thinking, or near to it, by the day you are married, then your friendship love will be strongly developed and you will be well set for a wonderful marriage together.

How far?

What about 'pre-marital sex'? Is intercourse all right in engagement? Entering into sexual intercourse before marriage – or cohabiting without intention to marry – seems almost the norm in this present age, but it seriously mars the growth of friendship love and goes deeply against God's best will for us. God is not a spoilsport, and was not ignorant of the possibilities of contraception! He is against sexual intercourse before marriage because he has a better plan. We will be happier if we hold back at this stage.

Some will argue that commitment is the key. They say that if you are committed to one another you can go ahead physically and then take the wedding service as a confirmation rather than a consummation. But the wedding *is* the commitment!

Others say that no 'red-blooded youth' can hold back. That really is absurd. We are both 'red-blooded' in this sense and held back (we are so thankful that we did). Restraint before marriage has not harmed our sex life – but rather heightened it as from the beginning it was the final consummation of our growing love, mutual respect, friendship and publicly affirmed commitment.

A man or woman who cannot have self-control is not truly a man or truly a woman since human beings have a mind and a will. John White in *Eros Defiled* (published by IVP) distinguishes between starving and fasting: if you are starving you can only think about food; but if you are fasting you turn your mind from it. He draws a parallel with fasting and chastity. Resolve to relate as persons not as sex objects. We would argue that those who enter into sexual intercourse before marriage have a low view of one another and of marriage and we believe in a high view – marriage is to be 'held in honour' (Hebrews 13:4).

Sexual intercourse binds you to the other – you become 'one body' and 'one flesh' (this happens even when intercourse is with a prostitute, says Paul in 1 Corinthians 6:16). Used to satisfy an appetite or indulged in as a normal part of courtship or engagement, it robs you of the superb sense of affirmation which should come in your total surrender to each other on your wedding night. God's intention is that you should be united to one another as 'one flesh' only when you leave your parents – not before (Matthew 19:5).

If you have already gone down the intercourse road, nothing can give you the full wonder of that experience as it should be after the wedding. But you may resolve to hold back from now until your wedding day so that something of what has been lost may be regained. It would be a mark of your respect for one another and, especially, for God's will and purpose if you followed this course – a path other couples have taken to their eventual joy.

The biblical advice to you if you really cannot contain yourselves physically is to marry (1 Corinthians 7:36). Although we

One mark of being right for each other will be a growing spiritual affinity.

advocate allowing time for your friendship to grow, you can have too long an engagement. To wait until you have 'saved up', or until a course has finished, or until the church or restaurant you want is available, is to put yourselves under unnecessary strain. An earlier wedding date may actually be a help rather than a hindrance to taking finals or facing uncertain financial situations. Love and obedience to God's will are more important than worldly considerations.

You may say: But isn't it different now that we've got safe sex? Doesn't contraception make everything all right since there's no risk of pregnancy?

But regardless of the question of whether any form of contraception is one hundred per cent 'safe', this objection does not change our fundamental point that sexual intercourse makes you 'one flesh'.

So, you may ask, how far can we go? The kiss, the embrace, the hug, the snuggling together on the sofa are good. They are a very important part of growing together. But if you go further – to the stimulation of sex organs, to 'sleeping' together without meaning to have intercourse, showering together in the nude and the like – you are unlikely to be able to stop. Once you are hotly aroused you will find yourselves going all the way – and bitterly regretting it afterwards. On the whole, a girl finds it easier to cope if she has not been deeply aroused, whereas since puberty the fellow has found himself rapidly aroused. So the restraint needs to be exercised more by the man than the woman.

By the day of the marriage your bodies will yearn for each other, and there will be no restraint, no secrecy, no sense of guilt, no need for rush, no risk and no disobedience to God when you come to the consummation of your commitment on your honeymoon (and then it does bring the honey and the moon!).

In December 1991 the bishops of the Church of England put it like this in their statement on marriage: 'God's perfect will for married people is chastity before marriage, and then a lifelong relationship of fidelity and mutual sharing at all levels.' The statement went on to recognise the difficulties in keeping this ideal when peer pressure is strongly opposed and urges uninhibited sexual intercourse even from puberty. Yet the report rightly points to the support to be gained from the fellowship of the church in maintaining 'the Christian vision for human life'.

God's best

If you really do want God's best, then you will be careful about your choice of friends at this time and you will share fully in church life and Christian fellowships. There is great value and encouragement in the friendship and advice of Christian couples already married. You can discuss with them the pressures to conform to non-Christian standards. You will also choose your films discerningly, you will avoid dressing in an overtly provocative way, and you will avoid putting yourselves into compromising or tempting situations. Aim at self-giving love and friendship love at this stage and you will find a growing fulfilment in your relationship, enormous fun and freedom plus a growing readiness for commitment and consummation. God's way is always the best.

We hope you have a lovely courtship and engagement. Growing together is to be enjoyed as well as worked at and needs to continue all your married life. Never stop courting!

Questions for discussion

Friendship, we have read, is vital for a marriage relationship to work and last. Consider your friendship and the priority you give it with your partner.

1. As you approach your wedding day, what is the most important aspect of your relationship together? If it is not your friendship, then discuss your priorities together. Do they need to change?
2. How can you make the most of the time before you are married? Having read about examples in the chapter, think about opportunities you could take in order to deepen your friendship. Why not make a list of things you would like to do and then plan together how you are going to achieve them?
3. If you are a Christian believer, how much of your faith are you sharing with your partner? Discuss together how you can best do this.
4. Having read about God's will for us and our marriage, consider your sexual relationship. If necessary, talk to each other about the past. Do you need to change the way you are relating to each other now? Discuss how you are going to save sexual intercourse for marriage – does your behaviour need to change?

4. Preparing for the Wedding

PRACTICALITIES – * Jump Chapters Four and Five if you are already married or are not yet ready for wedding details!

It is *your* wedding

You are the two who will say 'I will'; you are the two drawn together by love on this day. It is your wedding and you will be centre stage. Relatives and friends will naturally want to celebrate with you, but they should not control the details. On occasions we have seen the wedding taken over by the bride's mother, like a general commanding a major campaign, and the couple have hardly been consulted. On the other hand, we have seen couples ignore every request and suggestion from anyone else, and this has been hurtful (and usually not all that successful). It is certainly difficult for the bride's parents if they are expected to pay for the reception and yet have no say in the arrangements! The bridegroom's parents need to be included too, as they are just as involved emotionally in the delight of their son's marriage.

Thinking it through

We suggest you start *as a couple* in thinking through the general principles and pattern that you would like for the wedding and then have a family discussion, hopefully with both sets of parents present. Parents will normally want the best for you within their financial means, and they have understanding and experience. So do listen to them and be ready to adjust or compromise. Incidentally, it is usual these days for the parents of the bridegroom to make some contribution to the heavy cost.

This is going to be a family-and-friends occasion. You may wish

Start by thinking through the sort of wedding you would like.

to have a quiet wedding with very few present. You may be saying, 'There's no need for all that fuss!' But self-giving love on your part means that you accept your involvement with family and friends, that you do not minimise family love, that you enjoy giving your friends the joy of sharing with you. Our Lord certainly wanted the wedding at Cana of Galilee to be a success and took the trouble to be there (John 2:1–11). Like your parents, you also will need to give and take as a couple.

Arranging the date

The most important part of your wedding day is the wedding service. So you must begin your plans with the church. Do not, of course, book a reception or a honeymoon before approaching the minister of your church. You can be married in the church of the parish where either of you lives or where either of you is on the electoral roll. (For members of non-conformist churches this geographical restriction does not apply.) You cannot go out to find the prettiest church and book it like booking a restaurant. It is possible, under some circumstances, to seek an archbishop's licence to allow you to be married elsewhere, but the reasons for that cannot be because you like the church building!

If you live away from your family home but want to be married at that home you will need to return for some weeks to re-establish residence. You need to be clear about all this so that you do not approach a clergyman who, by law, will not be able to marry you in his church. When you have thought it through, arrange an appointment to go and see the minister. (Do not ring up expecting a wedding date to be given and fixed over the telephone.)

Meeting the minister

There may be a 'surgery' evening at your minister's house or office. Alternatively, he or she may fix a special appointment with you. At the first interview, you will need to check the qualifications for being married in that church – residence, electoral roll and the like. If you hope to be married in a non-conformist or Free Church, there will not be any hesitation if the minister knows you, but if you are strangers he or she will want to talk to you before deciding whether or not to marry you.

Then comes the matter of the date. There are so many events in a church's calendar and in a minister's life that the date and time may need quite a bit of negotiation (when we ministered near Manchester City football ground, the question whether the team was playing at home or away was a major influence on dates and times for weddings!).

Legalities and forms

In the Church of England the process usually begins with the filling in of a detailed form. This information will later be transferred to your marriage certificate, so go armed with correct details of your fathers' full names and occupations (we have seen arguments between father and son in the vestry after the wedding about the father's names!). Since these facts are needed for legal documents, accuracy is essential.

If your marriage is to be in an Anglican church banns will usually be called three times in both your parishes and, if you are on the electoral roll of yet another parish, there as well. More often than you would believe, couples forget to arrange for the reading of banns in the other parish(es) or forget to pick up the certificate(s) of banns after they have been read, failing to get them into the hands of the officiating minister before the wedding and so preventing the wedding from proceeding. The result is panic and a frantic attempt to get a licence at the last minute. The responsibility for getting those other banns called and the certificate(s) delivered is entirely yours.

It is good to be present when the banns are called – at least on one of the occasions, if the other church is far away. In most churches there is public prayer for couples who have had their banns read for the third time. The Christian fellowship is involved with you in desiring God's best for your marriage.

Preparation sessions

Most ministers will expect you to come to one or several preparation evenings. Some of these may be conducted by others experienced in marriage. Dr Jack Dominian thinks a six- to eight-week course should be mandatory, two hours per evening led by a team of lay people. (See *Passionate and Compassionate Love: A Vision for Christian Marriage* by Jack Dominian, Darton, Longman and Todd.)

We found it best to have several couples together, as that enables open discussion. It also means that subjects which some couples might hesitate to raise do get asked by others. Some ministers, however, arrange the preparation sessions with just one couple.

Preparation evenings are usually very valuable sessions and are to be welcomed rather than resented; it is, after all, a considerable giving of time and care by the minister or lay people. They are held out of genuine concern and Christian love in order to help you in the great adventure ahead. They also enable you and the minister to get to know one another. On the wedding day you will find you have a rapport and understanding which has arisen from these special times together.

Which service?

At one of those sessions with the minister you will need to sort out the details of the wedding service. If you are Church of England members you will no doubt be asked whether you want the 1662 Prayer Book service or the *Alternative Service Book* form. You will want to hear what the minister advises, but also you must read both services through carefully for yourselves – do not rely on the comments, prejudices or opinions of others. You will notice the considerable differences in the opening exhortation, in particular in the reasons given for marriage. You will also notice that in the *Alternative Service Book* both bride and groom have words for the giving of rings, and that when only one ring is to be given there are words for the receiving of the ring. Apart from the obvious contrast of Elizabethan and modern English, these are the main differences.

Choice of details

The minister will 'talk you through' the service to establish how many hymns you would like and what they should be. Do some thinking beforehand but get the minister's advice too. The opening hymn should be a Godward hymn of worship and the final hymn, a hymn of dedication in which you commit to God your new life together. The middle hymn(s) can be about marriage, faith, or life – they do not need to be addressed *to* God.

Then there is the question of what names to use (for example, whether you want to be John Henry . . . and Mary Rachel . . . , or simply John and Mary after the first promise – you can even have nicknames!).

In the *Alternative Service Book* you will need to choose between the A and B forms of vows (that is, whether you will love and cherish, or love, cherish and worship/obey).

Will you have one ring or two?

Would you like to sit for the address?

These are some of the things to get sorted out. Other possible details include:

- arrangements for an organist and possibly a choir;
- arrangements for flowers, when they can be put in and who can do them (and what happens to them after the service – usually they remain for Sunday worship);
- rules about access for the photographer and, if required, video cameraman – without disrupting the service; complications can arise here over copyrights, fees and permissions by the organist and others;
- rules about confetti;
- details of the overall fees for the wedding (these are modest compared with the cost of most receptions), and you may want to make a separate 'thank you' gift to the church as an offering to God.

Holy communion

Some couples may want to receive communion as part of the wedding ceremony. If so, it may be wise to restrict reception of the sacrament to yourselves or to yourselves and your immediate family. Otherwise, your non-Christian friends may feel alienated, and the balance of the service will be upset because of the length of time needed for all to receive. Naturally, you will need to talk this through carefully with your minister.

Rehearsal

Usually there will be a rehearsal before the wedding – preferably the day or evening before, as it is then usually possible for parents, bridesmaids, and best man to be present. This is of enormous help in making sure that everything runs smoothly on the day itself. Normally you will literally walk through the service from the bridegroom's arrival to the procession out. Points to have in mind will be covered when we discuss the wedding in the next chapter.

It really is worth every effort to get all the main participants present for this rehearsal, so fix the date and time for it when you fix the wedding date. It is a constant surprise to couples and other participants that being involved 'up front' is vastly different from watching from the congregation. Every minister has a string of stories about gaffes, mistakes and 'dramas' at weddings. We will never forget the couple who knelt on all fours like two poodles (joining their hands together was hilarious!). Nerves and tension are eased by a trial run, and the best man is reminded to bring the ring(s)!

Ready in spirit

If you have not been regular members of a church, this is a good time to go together to Sunday services in preparation for taking these great vows before God. Many couples have realised at this time that knowing and worshipping God needs to be a major part of their life together and have asked the minister to help them in this.

Your wedding service

You can get so caught up with the details, the arrangements and the flood of practicalities that when your wedding day arrives you can lose the major meaning of the service and find yourselves going through a form of words instead of coming together in the presence of God. Be aware of this danger and aim to take your vows in a spirit of worship and dedication to God, genuinely praying from the heart in the latter part of the service.

Try to give yourselves a proper rest. Working right up to the day before the service is not helpful. If you come to the service with all the detailed arrangements put to one side, your bodies rested and your minds peacefully and joyfully looking forward to your marriage before God, it will be a *very* special day.

Sorting out the other details

You will no doubt draw up your own check list. Here are some details to include on it:

If you have prepared carefully, it will be a very special day.

1. Reception
You will talk this through with whoever is going to pay! You do not have to 'keep up with the Joneses' by spending a small (or large) fortune. You may have different standards from your parents or other relatives if you are both Christians and they are not. This may raise the sensitive question of alcoholic drink – and how much of it. You will probably want to offer a choice of alcoholic and non-alcoholic drinks, but also avoid the ceremony degenerating into a 'booze-up' with the inevitably raucous consequences. Quite often these days there is a 'family-and-close-friends' reception in traditional style and then a wider, more informal gathering a little later for a much larger circle of friends.

2. Invitations and service sheets
You may want to have a service sheet printed – if so, make sure to get it checked by the minister. The invitations will need printing and an invitation list sorted out. If one family is much larger than the other take care to keep the number of invitations roughly equal, to avoid one family swamping the other. It will be helpful to include detailed travel instructions or maps for people coming from a distance.

3. People to participate
- Who is to be best man?
- Who are to be bridesmaids or matrons-of-honour, and perhaps page-boys and girls (be careful – young children can be angelic – but they can also wreck a wedding!).
- Who will make speeches at the reception?
- Who will you invite to be ushers at the service?
- What are the main participants to wear? If you are asking the ushers to wear morning suits – are you paying? Who is going to decide on, make and pay for the bridesmaids' dresses . . . and so on?
- What 'thank you' presents will you give to the best man and the bridesmaids?
- Do you know of a good photographer who will not cause a long delay before the reception?

4. Medical
Out of consideration for one another, ask your doctor for a medical check-up. You will be wise to talk through family planning together either with the doctor or at a family planning clinic.

It is good to think over your forthcoming privilege of sexual intercourse – reading, learning and talking together about it.

5. Church affiliation
If you are both members of the same church, then no discussion is necessary except on your choice of church, if you are beginning your married life in a new area. However, if you belong to different Christian denominations, what are you going to do in the future? Will you continue to worship separately? We hope not. Are you going to alternate? That is possible but limits your ability to contribute to one church as committed church members. Will you start attending a church of an entirely different denomination? That is possible but involves throwing away a lot.

The best course is for one of you to change denominations. If you make this decision it would be good to go through any preparation for membership before the wedding so that you can begin your married life as one in this. It is a lot to ask (we speak from personal experience) and may cause some heartache as you explain the reasons for changing to members of your home church, but in the long term it is right that you should be united in this way. If you have children, they will benefit from sharing naturally in that unity.

6. *Changing your name*

Although just occasionally a bride refuses to take her husband's name, this does cause endless fuss and confusion and raises a query over what you mean by becoming 'one'. So we hope you will accept the change, though it is never without some regret at first. However, it affects many documents – not least your passport. If you are going abroad on your honeymoon, you can get the passport changed beforehand. The minister signs the form and promises to tell the passport office if for some reason the wedding does not go ahead.

Then there are subscription registers, bank accounts, medical records, driving licence, insurance policies, membership of professional bodies, etc. Some wives retain their maiden name for professional purposes (actresses, artists, writers and so on). A quick run through all your papers will help you through most of the changes needed.

7. *Money, home and furniture*

Money is so important a factor in marriage that we give it a whole chapter later on. But at this point you need to decide whether you are going to have a joint bank account and joint credit cards, even if you retain separate personal accounts as well.

You will be planning where to live. It is important, if possible, that your home should be somewhere that is new to both of you. This is preferable to adapting either of the places where you live at the moment. You need to establish bit by bit what you both want your joint home to be like. It is also much better to be alone together in something uncomfortably small than comfortably with in-laws or friends. If you are content to live simply, rather than at a standard your parents have reached after twenty-five or so years of marriage, you will be happier – life is more than possessions. There is great enjoyment in getting a home ready (but it is also hard work).

8. *Spiritually*

Try to prepare yourselves spiritually for the wedding. It is good, when possible, to end your times together during engagement with prayer – particularly for the wedding itself, but also for your oneness in the marriage ahead. At the back of this book there are some Scripture passages you may like to read, with some prayers.

More important than every detail, every arrangement and even than your love for one another, is the Lord of creation, the Lord of the church, the Lord of all life – your Lord – and you need most of all to allow him to be Lord of your marriage. May you increasingly love him together, with all your heart, mind, soul and strength. Then on the great day of the wedding, whatever the weather, even if the arrangements are not perfect, as you are joined to each other, you will also be truly joined together to God.

Questions for discussion

It will be helpful to use this chapter as a check list, working through each detail and coming to a decision as to how it will work in practice at your wedding. Before doing that, however, consider the following questions:

1. Individually, think what your hopes and expectations are for the wedding day. It might be useful to write them down. Compare your ideas – are they similar or does some form of compromise need to be reached?
2. Anticipate how your family will react to your ideas for the wedding day. If there is potential for difference of opinion, how are you going to cope with that?

5.The Wedding

'Have a nice day' is an inadequate greeting for *this* day! We want to say, 'Have a wonderful, worshipful, joyful day – a day bathed in the richness of love and the outpoured blessing of God.' It should indeed be one of the loveliest days of your life.

Why have a wedding ceremony?
Surely, say some, there is no need. It is quite true that apart from the wedding at Cana of Galilee the Bible says little about such ceremonies. But probably this is because weddings were so much the norm that it would never have crossed anyone's mind that anything needed to be said.

Of course, in the physical sense you are married through sexual union – hence the possibility of annulment if the marriage is not consummated. But the wedding ceremony is the *public* declaration of the marriage. It marks the definitive start of your union, the start of the journey of your marriage and shared life as husband and wife.

Seeing people off on a journey is part of family love and care – waving from the dockside, the airport terminal roof, the railway platform or even the front door. We wave because we wish our relatives and friends well as they launch forth, and this is what is happening at a wedding.

It really is a lovely testimony to you both that many want to share with you, even just for the service if there are too many for the reception. They love you, value you and wish the very best for you. If you are members of the church, then many of your brothers and sisters in Christ will delight to be with you and pray for you. As you look at everyone on the way back down the aisle or at the reception, give thanks to God for your relatives (even for any you find difficult) and for your friends, and bask in their love for you.

Ushers at the ready

The ushers will not only need to be at the church in plenty of time, but also to be informed about their duties and the geography of the building. One usher should be made responsible for looking after any wedding gifts brought to the service by guests.

Arriving at the church

This needs careful timing. The bridegroom and best man normally arrive at least fifteen minutes beforehand and are usually asked to check the registers in the vestry.

The bride should aim to arrive with her father three or four minutes before the service is due to start. This allows time for the photographer to take arrival photographs, for the dress and veil to be arranged and for the bridesmaids and minister to be greeted. The old idea that the bride should keep everyone waiting is not fair on anyone, not on the minister, organist and choir, nor, of course, on the bridegroom, sitting conspicuously (with mounting tension!) at the front, nor on all your relatives and friends, who fidget and stare with increasing impatience.

A wedding that starts on time shows courtesy and respect for everyone waiting in the church. Sometimes traffic problems cause delays and these cannot be helped, although it is better to get in sight of the church and wait (or drive round it several times!), if traffic is likely to be bad. Get off to a great start by being on time.

The form of service

Services vary. We will take you through the service as it is in the *Alternative Service Book* because this is used at most Church of England weddings these days. The version in the *Book of Common Prayer* follows more or less the same pattern. Non-conformist churches follow it broadly, but with considerable variation of detail. It would help if you had an *Alternative Service Book* or, better still, two copies of the booklet containing just the marriage service (these are published separately) as you can mark them up for yourselves and even use them on the wedding day.

Starting the service

You will need to decide whether the bridal procession up the aisle should be with music or a hymn. We recommend music, as this gives you time to settle at the chancel steps before plunging into the promises. This way, the bridegroom and best man (on the bridegroom's right) go forward to the chancel step at the start of the music. Sometimes a bridegroom will turn and greet his bride as she walks up the aisle; others are too shy, as it means facing the whole congregation!

The bride, on her father's *right* arm, comes up the aisle with the bridesmaids behind (unless you prefer the American style of sending the bridesmaids up in front one by one). The bride arrives at the chancel step and hands her bouquet to the chief bridesmaid. Then the minister will usually say a word of welcome before announcing the first hymn. As the hymn is sung you both have the opportunity to settle into worship in preparation for the vows and promises.

After the first hymn

The bride's father, the bride, the bridegroom and the best man are standing in line at the chancel step (this is the order when looked at from behind). The bridesmaids usually remain standing behind you both. There is a Scripture sentence on God as love, and a prayer for your love. Occasionally there is a reading, followed by a sermon, but usually these come at a later point in the service.

At paragraph 6 comes the exhortation. The first time we used this and heard it we were moved to tears. It is superb. It covers friendship love, the love of family and friends, sexual love, and self-giving love. It reminds you that marriage involves the community and is not to be selfish. Marriage, it says, is part of God's creation purpose, but Christian marriage is highlighted – it is a means of grace; it is like Christ's love for his Church; it is so that children may be brought up in accordance with God's will. All this is in the context of the solemn statement that by his Spirit, Christ is with you in this very service.

Any objections

The minister is required by law to ask whether anyone knows any reason why you should not be married. It sounds foreboding and most ministers would not know what to do if any objection were raised! If there were any genuine reason, you yourselves would know and it would have been dealt with long before. However, if – and it is a very big 'if' – an objection was raised that seemed to have substance, the minister would have to announce an interval and then deal with the matter in the vestry. Do not worry – it has not happened in any of the hundreds of weddings we have been involved in (yet!).

The questions
Notice that the first question you are asked is about love. You are told that love for your partner involves 'forsaking all others' and being 'faithful to him/her as long as you both shall live'. The one leads to the other. There may be times when you feel attracted to someone else, but you are committed now to each other, and any other attraction must be 'booted into the stands' immediately. Your faithfulness to one another needs to be so complete that there is never a waver in your trust. Some wives feel insecure because they do not trust their husbands with secretaries or on business trips away, and some husbands feel insecure because their wives are highly capable. Your faithfulness should never be in doubt.

You are asked if you will 'comfort, honour and protect' your partner. These are ways of expressing your faithfulness, and are part of living through whatever life brings.

Having thought all this through beforehand, you should be able to answer 'I will', from the heart.

The promises
You now make the promises in turn. The bridegroom, with his right hand (his left hand is nearer to the bride so he needs to think 'right') takes the bride's right hand. How the holding is done (hands upward or downward) does not matter – it is the act of taking that is significant. Traditionally, the bride's father takes the bride's right hand (again, the left hand is the nearer and in the tension of the moment many fathers grab the wrong hand!) and puts her hand in the bridegroom's. If you would like to have the question, 'Who gives this woman to be married to this man?' (it is in the *Book of Common Prayer* version) you should ask whether this can be added.

Making the promises

Will you repeat or read the promises? Memorising is *not* advisable – it seldom succeeds and only adds tension to the ceremony. Repeating phrase by phrase after the minister is the traditional way (originating from the time when many people could not read). The words can still be repeated wrongly (one famous bridegroom in front of a huge worldwide television congregation endowed himself with his wife's goods and gave her none of his considerable wealth!).

The alternative is to read them 'solo'. We have found this to be preferred by most couples these days. You can, of course, read them straight from the book, but many couples find it better to write out the words separately, including the names, in large legible print on a card. These can be held by the minister or best man and father, or by yourselves.

The meaning of the promises

You are making the most far-reaching and deeply significant commitment of your lives to each other, whatever may come – 'for better, for worse, for richer, for poorer, in sickness and in health'. In these words you are facing anything that may happen and pledging your love as unbreakable (just as Christ's love for us cannot be broken – see Romans 8:38–9). You are also pledging to love and cherish 'till death us do part' (a phrase you might prefer to change to 'until we are parted by death'). This is God's intention for marriage. You must not enter marriage with any lesser aim.

Taking one another

After the bridegroom has made the promises you release hands and the bride takes the bridegroom's hand (with the same hands, but now the bride is doing the 'taking'). The fact that the bride in her turn 'takes' the bridegroom is important. You are both equal in the sight of God, you are both adults making a thought-through decision and you are each taking the other. Christian marriage is a partnership, not a take-over.

The rings and the declaration

The ring is 'a symbol of unending love and faithfulness'. It has no end. It has no corners. When you look at it on your finger it is a reminder to you of your promise. It is also an outward sign of the covenant, or agreement, made publicly between you both.

The best man usually holds the ring(s). He puts the ring (or both rings if there are two) on the book held by the minister. After a prayer you take the ring and place it on the fourth finger of your partner's left hand (a fact known, it seems, to every girl from a very young age and observed immediately at any party or gathering, but seldom known or even noticed by men!).

In the *Book of Common Prayer* version there are only words for the bridegroom to say but in the *Alternative Service Book* version both have words to say – the bride saying words to 'receive' the ring if only one ring is given, or to 'give' the ring if she is giving the man a ring as well. This is the point at which you pledge to honour one another with your bodies. The purpose and meaning of this is beautifully described in the opening exhortation: 'that with delight and tenderness they may know each other in love, and, through the joy of their bodily union, may strengthen the union of their hearts and lives'. Again, the words can be repeated or read.

The joining of the hands

The minister then joins your hands together (right hand to right hand again, even though the man's left is nearer) and declares you to be man and wife, with the added charge: 'That which God has joined together, let not man divide.' At that point your married life has begun. You are then blessed as husband and wife.

Concluding the service

In some churches the bride and groom, together with the parents, best man and bridesmaids, now go out to the vestry to sign the registers but usually this is done at the end of the service. If the custom is for it to happen here, then some anthem, solo or other music needs to be provided for your congregation.

The best man and bride's father return to the front pews. It is kind to let the bridesmaids sit down, too. If you would also like to sit down for the reading and sermon, agree on this beforehand so two chairs can be ready.

Many people have a hymn before the reading of Scripture and the sermon. Think about the Scripture reading you would like to have before you discuss it with the minister in marriage preparation. Often a relative or friend is asked to read.

Leaving and cleaving

There is provision for a hymn or an anthem after the address, and in churches with a chancel you follow the minister up to the communion rail at this point. In this way, you demonstrate that you are now a couple, the movement underlining the biblical requirement that you 'leave father and mother' and 'cleave' to each other. We will talk about this later as too many marriages are wrecked by parents not 'letting go' or by one or both partners in the marriage still putting parents before their spouse. This must not happen and you say so by this physical move together to the communion rail.

After the hymn, the minister will invite everyone to pray and you will kneel. The prayers chosen do not have to be the prayers in the service book – but you will see how lovely and relevant the service book prayers are. They cover the themes of spiritual grace, love and security, children, the home and sharing that home with others. We include some of them at the end of this book as they are suitable for praying before marriage, on your honeymoon – and always. You are clearly now committing your life together to God, seeking to be his in every way in your relationship to one another, to others and especially to your Lord and Saviour, Jesus Christ.

The service may end with those prayers and a blessing, or you may have a final hymn before the blessing.

In the vestry

Usually this is the point when you go to the vestry, or to a side aisle (but if this has happened earlier in the service you now turn to go down the aisle). Your best man, parents and bridesmaids go out with you to the vestry. On your return, your best man will walk back down the aisle with the 'chief' bridesmaid or 'matron of honour'. If there are also other adult bridesmaids, it is wise and sensitive to have a male consort for each of them. In this case, arrange in advance for ushers or male relatives to go to the vestry with you or to be ready to move from the front pews.

In the vestry you will both have to sign the registers (there are two). Your signature has to accord with your full names, in the bride's case, her maiden name (you must include *all* your initials or names) and as the registers are to be exact copies of each other, how you sign in one must be how you sign in the other. Sometimes the minister will get you to sign the copy certificate as well.

You have to provide two witnesses, who should be chosen and asked beforehand. Otherwise you have the embarrassing situation of everyone politely saying, 'Why not X or Y?' We have discovered, from long experience (!), that it is politic to choose someone from each family (fathers, mothers, brothers or sisters) or two people from neither family (best man and a bridesmaid).

The minister completes the certificate and hands it to the 'new wife' (it is the wife's property). There may then be some speedy photographs, after which you line up, men always on the right with their sword-arm free! Bridegroom and bride go first, of course, then best man and senior bridesmaid, other bridesmaids (and possibly consorts), the bridegroom's father and the bride's mother, and finally, the bride's father and the bridegroom's mother.

A signal to the organist and you are off! Revel in it. Come out and look your relatives and friends in the eyes! Share your joy and thrill at being married. Let the congregation know it!

After the service
Weather permitting, you now have photographs outside. Hopefully, the congregation will be able to leave the church by other doors so that they can enjoy this with you. Keep the photographer moving. Do not let him go on and on, as this will tarnish the joy and celebration. Then it is off to the reception.

It is a sign of thoughtfulness to ask the ushers to clear up the church after the service and try to pick up any confetti lying around. Quite often confetti is banned from the church precincts because it causes a terrible mess, especially if it rains.

Don't worry!
Do not worry about all the details of the service. Going through it as we have done, and as you will do with your minister, will prepare the way. On the day the minister will guide you at every point, so relax! It will be a great day – a wonderful day – so enter into it with joy, worship and love. Those are the essential ingredients – the rest will happen.

God bless you gloriously on your wedding day.

Questions for discussion

Once again you will find it helpful to use this chapter as a detailed check list. Why not read and consider each aspect together?

1. Do any aspects raise issues that need further thought or other advice or action?

2. How will you prepare *yourselves* for the wedding day – in mind, body and spirit, for example, a positive attitude to enjoy the day, rested and refreshed, praying for God's blessing?

3. Can you plan how to give yourselves to parents, relatives and friends so that they can fully share your joy on this day?

6. Adjusting to Being Married

Getting away

At last, you are alone together! After all the bustle of the days before the wedding, all the demands, joys and involvements of the wedding day, all the greeting of relatives and friends at the reception, you will be so thankful to be alone. That moment of waving the others goodbye and setting off is wonderful!

If you can have a honeymoon away, or even if it has to be at home, aim to be free of pressure about time. There is a sort of blissful timelessness in your new total relationship. Everything else is secondary. Your honeymoon helps you in adjusting to being married. It is a time of fun and discovery together.

The first year

From earliest times it has been recognised that the first year of marriage is very important. This is when you get to know one another; it is a time for adjustment and for sorting out your lifestyle, priorities and relationships.

Deuteronomy 24:5 says, 'If a man has recently married, he must not be sent to war or have any other duty laid on him. For one year he is to be free to stay at home and bring happiness to the wife he has married.' Splendid advice! Unfortunately, it is not possible to have a year off in today's world! However, the principle is important. You do need as much time together as possible in your first year so that your marriage may be well and truly built on strong foundations.

Your new life

Sharing with another human being in the intimacy of marriage involves every aspect of living. For a start, you have another body to care for as your own. You may have a thorough understanding of the body of the opposite sex from sex education lessons at school (though there is quite a gap between theory and practice in any learning). Or you may have grown up in a large family with brothers and sisters where understanding has developed naturally. However, if you have not had that background you may need to be helped to learn about the other's body.

To start with, initial intercourse can cause physical pain to the wife, and the husband must be gentle so that this lovely part of your oneness can develop without problems.

You may also need to talk about specific medical matters connected with your partner, especially where ongoing care or treatment is needed. You will then be able to offer help if needed.

Becoming a couple means much more than a new physical relationship, of course. Your marriage has not just made legitimate what was illegitimate before, but is the union of two persons, of all that you are. It includes your emotional and spiritual life, your character, skills, experience, intellectual ability, social relationships, physical looks, strengths and weaknesses. It is the security of your commitment which will enable you to help one another, to grow as persons and to assist any necessary healing of the past. In the relaxed joy and openness of the honeymoon you will find it increasingly possible to share thoughts and feelings, worries and fears, and incidents from the past that should no longer be kept to yourself.

It is a time of talking about the experiences and memories of life from your earlier years, sharing the joys and the problems of those years, the happy and the sad times, the successes and the failures. You are encountering one another as whole persons and the more you know about each other, the sooner you will have no secrets from one another. The greater your openness to one another, the more truly you become one in heart, mind, body and soul.

The 'soul' side of your relationship is the most important. You will need to learn to minister to, and be ministered to, in your spiritual growth together, and always to be rooted deeply in God's love. We talk about this later, but establishing this priority in your marriage needs to begin on the honeymoon.

If you can, go to a church on the first Sunday and share in holy communion together. In the context of worship, give thanks to God for one another and your privilege of marriage. If it is not possible on the first Sunday owing to travel, then establish the Sunday priority on the second Sunday of your married life. If there is no church nearby, hold your own service.

Take time on your honeymoon to think about chapter 11 of this book. And *from the first night,* let your Lord be Lord indeed of your marriage. End the day with prayer that night and *every* night of your married life. In your thinking and practice be clear that the Lord is the head of your marriage.

A fundamental switch

When you are first married there is a delight in speaking of 'my wife' and 'my husband' but learning to think and to speak automatically and normally in terms of 'we' and not 'I' takes quite a while. What needs to be expressed and experienced is a basic change of primary allegiance and responsibility.

Remember again the words of Scripture that 'a man will leave his father and mother and be united to his wife' (Genesis 2:24). The woman does the same. This is a considerable change, for the relationship with parents is deep even when it has not been smooth. The maternal bond is part of our very being by birth, a fact you realise as never before at the death of your mother. The paternal relationship is of a slightly different nature, but can run just as deeply. Strain or breakdown in those relationships does not take away their reality. So when you now switch your primary allegiance and relationship to your wife or husband it is a much more fundamental switch than you may at first have realised.

The switch has to be on both sides. Often it is the parents who find it more difficult to adjust. They are usually pleased to welcome a new son-in-law or daughter-in-law but inevitably see this as a family addition via their own offspring. The adjustment from a primary to a secondary relationship *must* be made, yet often it does not happen and demands, expectations and presumptions continue as if there had been no change. You have a problem, for example, or you fall ill, and your parents arrive to sort things out! It takes time for parents to learn that they may now offer to help but unless asked should never go further, and this calls for patience on both sides.

Do not cause friction in your new relationship as husband and wife by submitting to unfair expectations from parents – even though you want to go on loving them, respecting them and having an excellent relationship with them. For instance, parents who expect the newly-weds to come to their home for family lunch every Sunday are not being fair. Gently but carefully help your parents to adjust their thinking. Then you can develop your contacts with both sets of parents in an open and deepening way, with respect and mutual understanding, with care and love and with growing friendship.

In the same spirit, you must avoid 'ringing home to Mum' or 'having a word with Dad' whenever there is a problem, or even when there is not (some newly-weds seem to ring parents every day and even several times a day!). First try and work through problems together. This does not mean that you are cut off from parental care, support or advice, but that parents are no longer to be the first line of consultation – although often they will naturally be the second.

One of the biggest causes of friction in the early years of marriage is over this matter of 'leaving and cleaving', so it is important to work at it from the beginning. The new relationships must be clearly established.

Your friends

Most adjustment in the early part of marriage involves a working out of the biblical principle that 'in the Lord woman is not independent of man, nor is man independent of woman' (1 Corinthians 11:11). This refers to life in general but becomes particularly relevant in marriage.

It is true, as we shall discuss later, that your love for each other must not be selfishly exclusive, and that it will go sour if it does not have other friendships. You must be ready to give to others and serve them, and allow room for separate personal development. Yet it is also true that you cannot simply go on with all previous friendships and relationships as if nothing had changed. The new husband who expects to go out alone with his mates several nights a week just as he did before he got married, has not made the change. You are not independent of one another.

Getting to know each other's friends is part of making the change. You may also need to be selective, and decide together which friendships should continue and which not. Otherwise, if

Getting to know each other's friends is part of making the change to married life.

you each come with large numbers of friends, you will be swamped by the combined number! It is particularly helpful to start making *new* friends *as a couple*.

Your new home

As we have already seen, in chapter 4, you should do your utmost not to begin your married life living with in-laws. Better to live in the smallest of apartments in spartan style than in comfort in a family home where your leaving and cleaving is not given a chance.

Setting up home together is fun but is also demanding, especially if you have not had your own flat or apartment before and have come straight from the family home to marriage. You will have taken much for granted over the years, unless you have been well and truly made to take a full share in the running of your family's household. Choosing colours and furniture is the pleasant part; the routines of putting rubbish out, cleaning, shopping, mending fuses, paying bills, keeping the home warm, cooking, washing up, laundry, gardening, repairing leaking gutters, wiring plugs, making curtains, mending clothes, entertaining, keeping the expenditure below income and all the other countless things that are part of domestic reality loom large and are not always so pleasant.

Now if you run out of milk there is no one else but yourselves to blame. There is no one else to iron endless shirts or paint the ceiling. Tension can be created by unrealistic expectations of what your partner should do. Beware of basing your ideas on parental or other role models when your partner's gifts or experiences are very different. With grace, positive thinking and a sense of humour it can be worked out and even enjoyed but when your growth in self-giving love is limited, different expectations can be a cause of friction. 'We' thinking can redeem the situation.

Settling down into being married takes time at all levels of your relationship. We look at some of the details in the rest of this book, but do realise now that the *slightly* rocky road in the first year is because you are walking along an unmade road. The more you adopt this new way of life and adapt to it, the more you find that the pot-holes disappear and the going becomes smoother. The more you can get beyond the feeling of being over-stretched by daily practicalities, the more you can develop the richer and fuller joys of being man and wife together.

Questions for discussion

So the wedding day is over and you are married. How will you find the early weeks and months?

1. Think over plans for your first year of marriage. Have you allowed for time together – how many evenings will you be at home? How often do you have visitors? Discuss strategies for protecting your time alone together.

2. Consider your relationship with your parents and parents-in-law. In the light of what you have read, do you envisage potential problems? How will you address these?

3. What do you see as your partner's domestic strengths and weaknesses? How do these compare with your own?

7. One Flesh

The sex factor in marriage is the most sublime expression of mutual love and self-giving available to human beings. It is the climax experience of total commitment and those who have sexual intercourse outside marriage abuse this, marriage's deepest significance. As a university chaplain used to say to his students: 'Sleep together only if you have a joint bank account – and you will do that only if you are totally committed – so marry!'

Eros

Much unhealthy emphasis is put upon the sex act. Books, magazines, films, television plays and pop songs promote the idea of 'sex for all'. As a result our views can easily become warped and tainted, even to the extent that we recoil from sex. When Hebrews 13:4 says, 'Marriage should be honoured by all and the marriage bed kept pure,' the writer is referring to the essential commitment of the married couple which is not to be wrecked by adultery. However, the Greek word translated here as 'kept pure' means 'untainted by the world' when used by James (James 1:27) and it is this tainting from media and peer-groups that can seep into our attitudes and even into the love-act.

'Making love' is an inappropriate phrase if used for *any* sex act. It devalues the word 'love'. The physical union of our bodies is part of the natural instinct we share with the animal kingdom and is not in itself 'making love'. It is the commitment of deep love as the context for the act that transforms it into something gloriously wonderful which is then rightly called 'making love'. This is 'Eros' – true sexual love. Thought about in the abstract it can seem clinical, even repulsive; thought about as it is experienced, as an expression of true love, it is beautiful and rapturous – enveloping you until it takes you beyond word or thought.

The primary intention of marriage is companionship.

The primary intention of marriage is companionship (in Genesis 2:18 God said, 'It is not good for the man to be alone,' and he made Eve). Sexual intercourse is first of all for that purpose, for deepening the couple's relationship of love. If this were not so, God would not have allowed this part of our being to go on with vigour and ardour well beyond the years of child-bearing into our fifties, sixties and seventies (we are so glad that is so!). The *secondary* purpose is that of procreation – the privilege and awesome responsibility of giving birth to a new human being.

The balancing of these two purposes is much easier now than it was in the years before good contraceptive facilities. These have brought greater freedom and peace of mind than was possible when it was necessary to rely on 'safe days' in the month or on earlier forms of contraception. We do not, like some in the church, regard these as non-Christian or outside God's will. Rather, we see them as a major help in the enrichment of marital love through physical union. We think this even though the same methods have encouraged some people to indulge in sexual intercourse outside marriage and thus abuse its meaning and purpose. So be thankful for contraception, as it enables you to love one another more freely.

Love-talk and love-action
A good introduction to the 'language of love' would be to meditate on the Song of Solomon (the Song of Songs) in the Old Testament. What God has given us is beautiful but, because the 'world's' unhealthy attitude can contaminate us, we may not at first be at ease with such intimate language. Try reading the Song of Solomon together, thanking God for the beauty and wonder of physical love.

> 'My lover is to me a sachet of myrrh resting between my breasts' . . . 'How beautiful you are, my darling! Oh, how beautiful! Your eyes are doves' . . . 'Like an apple tree among the trees of the forest is my lover among the young men' . . . 'My lover is mine and I am his' . . . 'Your lips are like a scarlet ribbon, your mouth is lovely' . . . 'Your two breasts are like two fawns . . . that browse among the lilies' . . . 'My lover is radiant and ruddy . . . his arms are rods of gold . . . his mouth is sweetness itself; he is altogether lovely' . . . 'How beautiful you are and how pleasing, O love, with your delights! Your stature is like that of the palm, and your breasts like clusters of fruit. I said, "I will climb the palm tree; I will take hold of its fruit"' . . . 'Your mouth is like the best wine' . . . 'I belong to my lover, and his desire is for me.'

This language of love – an intimate and private language you will develop for yourselves – forms part of the foreplay of love.

The importance of foreplay is seldom understood at the beginning of marriage and there is – naturally enough – a tendency to rush things, particularly by the man. This is partly due to the fact that a man is easily and rapidly aroused and if he cannot divert his mind to another subject or find relief in some way the effect upon his sex organs is powerful and even painful. Women who have not had brothers will need to know this and to understand that the need for relief causes involuntary night-time emission of semen through erection in a man's sleep – a safety valve. It is part of the way men's bodies are made. Arousal can be instant.

Women are not aroused with the same speed. The build-up may be far longer (taking hours – even as long as twenty-four hours) and comes with the sense of being drawn to the man through his gentle encouragement, his touch, embrace and thoughtfulness, or after a lovely evening out together or some shared enjoyment.

When desire builds up towards a coming together, both partners will give indications of readiness – through touch, kiss, embrace and responsiveness. The build-up goes on from there, often continuing with the undressing of the other, and moves through an extended time of love-talk and love-action towards the climax.

The love-act loses its sparkle if it is routine. There needs to be variety about it. This is true of the technique; it is also true of the place (it does not need to be only in the bedroom) and the time of day. This freedom and variety will help when you have children, since finding a time when they will not walk into your bedroom may be difficult (and become increasingly difficult as they get into their teens).

Privacy is an important aspect of relaxing together in love. You need a locked door, the phone off the hook, the curtains drawn – and time. You may not mind if others knock on the door to ask a question, or hear everything through the bedroom wall, but most couples find their progress to the climax far from satisfactory under such conditions. Whenever possible you need to be truly alone and that may sometimes be easier in the day rather than the night. Such flexibility and variety are all part of the joy.

C. S. Lewis in his *The Four Loves* has a delightful description of the way in which the physical attraction (which he calls 'Venus') can 'make game of us':

When all external circumstances are fittest for her service she will leave one or both lovers totally indisposed for it. When every overt act is impossible and even glances cannot be exchanged – in trains, in shops and at interminable parties – she will assail them with all her force. An hour later when time and place agree, she will have mysteriously withdrawn; perhaps from only one of them.

How right he is!

You may know all there is to know about the sex organs, but a lot of couples do not. There are various books on the sex factor in marriage and the techniques of sexual intercourse, and these will give you more detail than is possible in the scope of this book. One such book is *Intended for pleasure – sex technique and sexual fulfilment in Christian marriage* by Ed and Gaye Wheat (published by Scripture Union). For those without much knowledge on the subject, basic information is given in the boxes below.

Reaching a climax

The object of the physical union is to help one another to achieve orgasm. It is also for the male's seed (sperm) to unite with the female's egg in the starting of a new life.

The man's sex organs

The man's sex organs are outside his body so that the sperm manufactured in his testicles can be at a suitable temperature. The number of sperm produced is in terms of millions. Above the testicles is the penis, which is normally quite small, but when aroused can rapidly extend to a considerable size, protruding from the body.

In ejaculation (which can happen unconsciously in sleep or by stimulation, as in the process of sexual intercourse) the sperm rises up the urethral tube into the penis and out from it – huge numbers of sperm in a milky liquid produced by other glands.

The tip of the penis is its most sensitive part. Some men are circumcised – which means that the foreskin has been cut back permanently, leaving the sensitive part exposed; others have to learn to ease the foreskin back frequently in washing so that it can happen easily for intercourse.

The woman's sex organs

The woman's sex organs are, of course, inside her body. The vagina is several inches long and has muscular walls that can expand (they need to stretch considerably when a baby is being born). The vagina is built to receive the penis and in that time of reception the couple are truly 'one flesh'.

Beyond the vagina is the womb, and connected to the womb by the Fallopian tubes are the ovaries which make the eggs. For conception to happen the man's sperm has to get into the womb and fuse with an egg. In the vagina are glands which, if there is proper fore-play, will be stimulated to lubricate the vagina (sometimes, especially later in life, lubricating fluid needs to be used).

In front of the vagina there are the visible 'outer lips', and then inner lips, the latter containing the clitoris which, like the man's penis, responds to stimulation. Usually the man stimulates the clitoris with his fingers after he has aroused his wife by kissing and then caressing the breasts and other parts of her body.

Stimulating one another to achieve orgasm (an experience like no other, when you are utterly 'taken over' by the climax of love) is something you will learn together. Do not take it too seriously, with endless detail in your heads and a desire for 'perfect' technique. Some only find the best approach when they throw the sex-technique books away and concentrate on what most helps and pleases their partner. This will involve experiment and use of different positions. Although the man lying on the woman is the norm, it can be anything but normal for some, especially if the man is very heavy. Some use the method of the man lying on his back and the woman sitting across him with his legs around her, and others use the side by side method, but many more positions are possible. All this is often quite funny – and laughter is better than tensed-up seriousness. Looked at in theory it is an extraordinary thing to do. In practice, in the warm light of love, it is sublime!

Once you have both experienced orgasm, you will want to be quiet together – to bask in the after-glow of this superb totality of union. This quiet, gentle time is like floating on air or being bathed with warmth. You feel you never want to part. Then it fades and surprisingly you can revert fairly rapidly to the other processes of living, though with some special cuddles along the way. If you have intercourse at night in bed, the man will afterwards often drop off to sleep almost at once (not very romantic!). The woman will take longer to 'cool down', just as she did to warm up.

It is important to approach love-making with careful hygiene – you owe it to each other. After intercourse there can sometimes be a seepage of semen back from the vagina, and you may like to have a cloth, handkerchief or towel at hand.

Problems
'Making love', as we have sketched it, happens easily for some couples and their openness in love sorts out any hiccups along the way; but this is not true for all couples. If you hit snags and problems, do not think you are exceptional and therefore do not be shy or reticent about getting help. Sadly, some Christian couples have such a spiritual outlook on life that talking about problems of this kind does not seem quite right to them. Yet God gave us our bodies and a Christian couple ought to act rapidly and purposefully to get to the state of physical union their Lord intended – except, of course, in the rare event that there is a fundamental medical problem that cannot be cured.

Start with your doctor and get advice about the next steps to take. There may be tension that tightens up the woman and prevents intercourse; or the man may have problems with premature ejaculation, or even in having an erection; or there may be long delay in conception; or there may be several miscarriages (which we had to face and so we understand the heart-pain when you wonder whether you can ever have a child). There may also be deep psychological bruises from childhood experiences that will need skilled counselling before sexual intimacy can be enjoyed.

Good and sensitive help, treatment and advice are available. Find it, take it – and be patient.

Problems in making love will also occur if your relationship is marred in other ways and, if so, other couples you know and trust may be the ones to help. Just one word of warning. There are some bizarre sex counsellors around who will suggest actions well outside Christian moral limits. If you find your counsellor is like that, then change to another – preferably one whom others can recommend.

Sometimes the husband or wife will not tell the partner about the problem so as not to cause hurt or disappointment. For example, the wife may never achieve orgasm; or the husband may find it extremely difficult to forbear if, for medical reasons, his wife needs to refrain from intercourse for a while; or one of the partners may react against the sexual relationship. It is, however, better to share these problems than to hide them. If suppressed, they smoulder away inside, and that is both dangerous and unnecessary.

We have to recognise that if 'cold' times come the cause will not normally be physical, and other reasons need to be looked at. It is important that you do not insist on conjugal rights, even though those rights have biblical warrant (1 Corinthians 7:3), because this is to treat your partner simply as a sex instrument. That is not Eros love, but is merely the satisfying of a physical need.

Recently the forcing of conjugal rights by a man against his wife's wishes has been designated as rape. You will never get to that point, we hope. The situation will not arise if in the rest of your married life you are growing together in love. So be the greatest of lovers!

Total joy

It is the loveliness, the beauty and the joy of sexual union that we want to underline. As C. S. Lewis put it in *The Four Loves*: 'Eros thus wonderfully transforms what is *par excellence* a need-pleasure into the most appreciative of pleasures.' This is because the whole context of the act is one of self-giving love, of total surrender to one another, of affirmation that each is to the other the most important and lovely person in the world. You have each gained a body; you each now have a male and female body as your own to enjoy, handle and hug. The penis and the vagina are for no one else – they are intimately, entirely and jointly yours. As a cartoon put it, the response of a grandfather to his grandson's question about what he wore to prevent getting any sexual disease was 'a wedding ring'.

You are exclusively each other's. You express it in the encouraging, appreciating, delighting, looking, touching, kissing and hugging that bring arousal and lead, as the marriage service put it, to 'know[ing] each other in love'. All barriers are removed, they are stripped in your total self-giving. As you share the language of love, you bring each other to orgasm in sexual oneness. Thank God together for the wonderful way in which you are made and thank him for giving you the joy and privilege of knowing the ultimate expression of love: becoming 'one flesh'.

Questions for discussion

Today, in society, sex is given disproportionate emphasis. Are your views and thoughts balanced or are they distorted and influenced by what you see and hear?

1. Read the Song of Songs. Does the language surprise you? Did you expect to find it in the Bible? Does it change your view of sexual love?
2. Have you considered the sexual differences between men and women? Does this affect how you approach your physical union together?
3. The chapter touches on problems that sometimes occur between couples. Do any of these concern you? Do you need to seek help from anyone at this stage of your marriage?

8. Give and Take

Now you are one. That is a fact. Yet, like oneness in the fellowship of the church, it needs to be worked out in practice, as St Paul says to the Christians in Ephesus: 'Be completely humble and gentle; be patient, bearing with one another in love. Make every effort to keep the unity of the Spirit through the bond of peace. There is one body. . .' (Ephesians 4:2–4). So marriage also has to be worked at with 'every effort to keep the unity'. For that to be achieved you need considerable give and take.

A dose of reality

You are both in love and you know that the heart of that love is *agape* (self-giving love) which involves wanting the best for your partner. If you are both Christians, then you know Christ and his love for you. This inspires you in your love for others and especially for one another. Yet the reality is that you are still people with a sinful nature within you and the wrestling between the Spirit and the flesh, or sinful nature, about which Paul writes is always going to be there (read, for example, Romans 7:7–25 and Galatians 5:16–23).

It is a paradox that the more you grow as a Christian, the more clearly you see sin in its multiple manifestations. All this is immensely relevant to your partnership together. Your 'new nature' wants to express and live by self-giving love, but your 'old nature' wants to act out of sheer self-interest. Your 'old nature', for instance, can persuade you that any manipulating of your partner to achieve a self-centred aim is simply a matter of commonsense and calls only for self-giving by the partner. It is a subtle

For marriage to work out, you need considerable give and take.

temptation and you may need to help one another to discern it, although pointing it out *at the time* may not be the most politic course to follow!

Sharing intimately as a couple exposes the areas where we have been self-centred. In *The Marriage Builder* (published by Zondervan), Lawrence J. Crabb Jr writes:

Merely changing what we do will not change who we are. The cure for the selfishness and fear that controls so much of what we do cannot be reduced to shallow solutions; we need to learn how our minds deceive us. We need to understand the wrong goals we have set, honestly face how we feel, and deal with our sinful and painful emotions in a way that reflects our confidence in God's unconditional acceptance.

Recognising that you are both saints *and* sinners will avoid your having a rosy picture of a perfect partner and of a perfect and unruffled relationship, where the sun always shines and soft music plays. We are not like that individually or corporately. If we realise this from the outset, we will want to begin the process of give and take. It is a two-way process that makes allowances for the frailty of the human spirit. Yet if we persist we will find that gradually over the years it will become less of a problem as we settle more into a partnership. As Dr Jack Dominian writes in *Passionate and Compassionate Love: A Vision for Christian Marriage*:

Little by little we become more resilient, our patience grows, we quarrel less and make up more quickly. We learn to see things from the point of view of our partner and our children. We give in without feeling humiliated or defeated.

When you come to marriage you have behind you, perhaps twenty, twenty-five, thirty or more years of single life, first as children, then as teenagers and adults, with growing independence and the establishing of your own personality, character and ways of doing things. Partnership, therefore, involves a colossal sea-change in your outlook. The older you are at the point of marriage, the more established you are in your life-style, habits, attitudes, opinions and ways of coping with the day-to-day needs of living. One of the great surprises of marriage – and one which is better treated as a cause of laughter and teasing than of criticism or stubbornness – is that your partner also comes with an established pattern, one that varies from yours in multiple ways, not least in the small routine habits of living. Unless you learn to give and take from the start you can become needlessly irritated.

Battle stations

One couple we knew had difficulty with their marriage within a year of their wedding. When they married they were both well beyond their thirties and had become very established in their single life-styles. The wife was immensely tidy – everything folded, put away in drawers, clothes taken off carefully and placed neatly or hung up in the wardrobe. That had been her daily pattern. The husband was completely untidy. Things were left all over the place. In particular (and this infuriated his wife) he undressed at night by taking garments off as he walked around the flat, dropping them on the floor wherever he happened to be at that moment. In the morning it had been his habit to retrace his steps and put his clothes on again in reverse order. Neither would yield; both insisted on their own way. Their marriage was at breaking-point.

We felt like knocking their heads together. We tried to get through to them that self-giving love demanded that they reach out and please the other. We said to the wife, 'Why did you not strew your clothes all over the flat?' and to the husband, 'Why did you not fold your clothes up neatly? You would then have had a good laugh at each other and would have reached a workable compromise.' It seemed unbelievable that two adult people could wreck their marriage over such a simple matter. Yet we know that this sort of unnecessary friction is commonplace. Almost always it is because there has been no give and take from the beginning: no partnership can survive and deepen without a lot of it.

Family traditions

The range of differences is far wider in scope than you might expect. The wife comes, say, from a family where the tradition has been for everyone to be in for steak-and-kidney pie on a Saturday lunchtime, while the husband comes from a family where they are all out most Saturdays and never have lunch together. Again, one partner may inherit a tradition of Christmas celebrations in which there is present-giving on Christmas Eve, a midnight service, and a lie-in on Christmas morning, followed by all the relatives arriving for lunch. But in the other family presents are always given after Christmas Day lunch when everyone has returned from the morning service; then it is just the immediate family on Christmas Day, with other relatives coming on Boxing Day. Deep down this has become the way each thinks it is 'right' to celebrate the festival.

Similarly, there may be different traditions about holidays – one family always goes to a hotel in the same place every year in Britain, and the other travels abroad to new places with a motor-caravan.

We inherit the traditions and ways of our family and they mould our unconscious attitudes. Somewhat irrationally, we regard these traditions as unchangeable. Love will enjoy experiencing the other's traditions and in your partnership you will begin to establish your own pattern together. This can be creative and uniting rather than destructive and dividing. You draw on your separate experiences and they enrich your joint decisions. But it requires give and take.

Habits

Personal habits can also be unexpectedly different. We may have been rather spoilt in childhood or brought up strictly; we could perhaps take a bath and leave a dark rim round the bath tub which our mother would come and clean or we may have been told to clean the bath after using it; we may never have helped very much in the kitchen and in domestic chores or we may have been expected to play a full part in the house; we may always have received the food we like or we may have been helped (cajoled?!) into exploring other foods and learned to eat whatever we received with gratitude and no complaint; we may have bathed or showered every day or we may have done so only once a week; we may have been late to bed and late getting up in the morning or early to bed and early to rise; we may have always worn night-clothes in bed or we may have slept naked; we may have let others make sure that our clothes were clean or we may have assiduously washed and ironed our own clothes; we may have been able to spend freely on clothes and on expensive foods or we may have had to use money carefully, with selective buying and a simple style of eating; we may be unconcerned about our figure or increasing weight or we may be figure- and weight-conscious with a healthy-food diet;

Each of you brings to the marriage a range of experiences from the past.

we may be used to a home which is vacuumed and dusted every day or one in which the state of cleanliness is unimportant.

From the start of your marriage you will recognise differences like these. Love will want to adjust so that your habits and ways do not conflict or irritate, even if some of them remain as your own style. Love will cause the phrase: 'But in our family we always. . .' to freeze on the lips. Wherever possible you need to establish a joint way of living until you have your own acceptable life-style as a couple. From the beginning this calls for give and take.

The new home

Setting up home can reveal further differences. Again, there may be quite a lot of influence from your upbringing as well as from the development of your individual tastes as you have admired other people's homes or experimented in furnishing a house or flat of your own. You both need to be happy with *your* home and this requires more than a mere compromise. Give and take will require some positive and creative thinking and sharing.

We ourselves have different artistic talents. At first our choices of furniture were limited both by the relatively narrow range in the shops in the 1950s, and by lack of finance. As both choice and finance have become greater we have had the fun of establishing our own styles. However, usually this has not been by the method of one saying: 'I like it, we'll have it,' but by our searching around in shops and catalogues until we both could genuinely say, 'That's it.' In this way our home is not a compromise, but a confluence of our tastes, representing what delights us both. As we have lived all our life together in tied houses it has been a particular joy in latter years to decorate and furnish our own retirement home in the style we jointly want from top to bottom.

The past

Each of you brings to the marriage a whole range of experiences from your past – some of them painful, others joyful. One may have had a bruised upbringing or been heavily disciplined and restricted; the other has perhaps had a wholesome upbringing, where a certain measure of discipline was always matched by much love and encouragement. One may have already lost a parent – or both parents – with deeply felt consequences, and may have had illness or seen a younger relative die or suffer, learning in this way to care and to understand pain; or there may have been no experience of pain, suffering, illness or loss, resulting, perhaps, in a lack of understanding and sympathy. One may have had to take the lead in the home, in sport or in a career; the other may not have had any leadership experience (this can happen, of course, either to the man or to the woman).

These backgrounds naturally affect our relationship in marriage and the more we know about each other's background the more we will understand 'where the other is coming from' in the working out of our relationship. This will often need to be a healing experience; it needs give and take.

Roles

The traditional roles of husband and wife are rightly challenged in our day. In the past the husband was the leader, the wage-earner, the doer of odd-jobs around the house, the carer for the fabric of the home, the handler of heavy jobs; the woman stayed at home to look after the house, to shop, prepare the food, clean the house, and not only bear children but be largely responsible for their care and upbringing. This can work very well. Proverbs 31 has a description of the good wife who fits the traditional stereotype (she may even have started it!). She is an excellent carer, bargainer and administrator and is at the forefront of charitable action to those in need. 'She is clothed in strength and dignity'; she has great wisdom and kindness. Her children 'arise and call her blessed', as does her husband, who 'praises her'.

The wife of Proverbs 31 is a very fulfilled person and this has been and remains true in many wonderful marriages. It will be particularly true where the husband offers great encouragement and appreciation of all that his wife has to handle, and is constantly ready to support the purchase of chore-saving equipment – washing machines, dishwashers, time-saving cookers and the like – but above all where he shows much understanding and love.

However, this is not the one and only pattern (and never has been). As different backgrounds and skills are brought to marriages today, few of which were possible in earlier generations, the roles of husband and wife may adjust and follow different patterns. Modern birth-control methods have also brought a far greater freedom to the wife, and greater opportunity to use her skills and talents. A woman who has trained as an engineer is more likely to be the practical one around the house; the man who has had training and experience in catering will take the major share of cooking. The woman who is an accountant will naturally handle finances, insurance and the like if her husband is not so trained – or even if he is. Either may be better at decorating, gardening, driving or bargaining. As we recognise each other's abilities and skills, there needs to be give and take.

As time goes on, and we see more clearly what each is good at, we may even think our partner is opting out if he or she does not bother with what has become 'yours to tackle'. In our own marriage one of us loves timetables, travel-planning and discovering the best fares, routes and bargains for holidays – it has become a form of relaxation – while the other delights in this and enthusiastically enjoys the results. One of us is far more ready than the other to try new things – foods, leisure activities, gadgets, skills and so on – and the other is glad not to be the pioneer but is happy to benefit from and praise the results. We both enjoy this give and take.

Earning a living

A wife may nowadays be more professionally qualified than her husband. Both will probably have careers or jobs, possibly positions of responsibility, and be respected in their own right at work, and with their own circle of colleagues and other friends. So what happens at marriage?

Normally both continue to work for a while, but this requires maximum sharing in the running of the home. A wife cannot be expected to have a full-time job and do all the shopping, washing, cleaning and cooking. It wrecks any real free time together and turns life into a treadmill. That is not right. If you are both going to work full time you *must* work out a pattern to minimise domestic chores (perhaps paying someone else to clean the house or to assist in the washing and ironing), eating out together more and *jointly* sharing in the shopping and all the domestic routine.

You must also try to coordinate your timetables so that you have free time together. Shift work can make that a problem but it can also make it easier. Never forget that your marriage is more important than status in the world or success in your career. If you can manage a career and keep growing in your love together, that is fine; but if your marriage development is being stunted, put on the brakes. One of you should perhaps go part-time if you can, or the right decision may be for only one to continue in a career. This becomes the pressing question in relation to having children. It can be a hard area of give and take for some (though by no means all) couples.

Starting a family

For financial reasons it may be necessary to delay having a family. Also, if possible, you do need to allow a period of time for settling into marriage before you start a family. The arrival of children is, as we will see in a later chapter, a revolution in both your lives. For the wife it can be an overwhelming change. Usually her career has to be set aside, even if only temporarily. Instead of going off to work and, in many cases, acting in a mentally exacting executive position, she is 'stuck' at home, responding to the endless night and day demands of the baby, with little to stretch her mind apart from all the 'how to bring up a baby' books, and questions of the right baby foods, the daily walk with the pram or pushchair, the

The arrival of children brings a revolution in your lives.

best toys, clothes, nursery schools, and so on.

Attitudes make the difference. It is possible to be so thankful for the joy of a child, so delighted at being a mother and so happy to be free of career demands that this becomes a lovely time in married life and a time when you make new friends, with other young mothers. What really helps is the 'give' of the husband, in immense thoughtfulness, in help with the practical tasks of baby-caring (especially at night) but most of all in ensuring that there can still be windows in your life – opportunities to stretch your mind, and to use your career skills. He will help you to find times when you can go out together while a relative or friend baby-sits, as well as making sure that you are often together as a family in your church and social life.

So the talented wife may be able to take the opportunity to be an examiner or marker of exam papers at home; or take a special assignment from her earlier career be it, say, as a musician, or accountant; or get the occasional duty back in nursing or retailing; or set up a business from home. This is something to explore together, and the husband will need to be a great encourager.

A wife can easily lose her sense of self-value, of self-respect and purpose in the early years of bringing up children. This must not happen. So think it through as the years go on. For us it proved a good step when Myrtle was able to do some part-time teaching again, first of immigrants needing to learn English, and then later in London when she set up a school in a large hospital. It did not take too many hours, the money was welcome and, more than all of that, she gained a group of colleagues and friends who were separate from our home and church and who valued and respected her, as she them. The decisions about her doing this were made together, as they always must be, for this is an area affecting both partners in, for instance, daily timetable, use of car, and family and domestic responsibilities. It is a major area of give and take.

Personal space

However much you love each other and become increasingly a loving and successful partnership, you are still individuals, and it is good to recognise the need for space in your marriage. It is important that you can at times be alone – free to enjoy a sport as participant or spectator, to pursue a hobby or visit the shops, go to a film or meet friends. This is especially true when you are both highly intellectual or have strong characters.

It helps both partners when one says, 'I'll look after the children today while you go off for your favourite pursuit,' and it strengthens rather than weakens togetherness. Some couples like to have separate holidays, perhaps because they have very different ways of relaxing, or because one does not like travel and the other does. Personally, we could not think of holidaying apart. Yet we have learnt the value of enjoying separate activities, with one of us going off to tennis tournaments while the other goes elsewhere at other times. If your tastes do not meet, for example, over music, you may need space to enjoy your preferences alone – and the other partner may be glad not to have to endure them! It is a matter of give and take.

There is really no need for your marriage to run into troubled waters in its first years, even though your differences may constantly surprise you. Maximise strengths and minimise weaknesses by sharing responsibilities accordingly. Keep on adjusting. Your love for one another, and your shared love for God, are paramount. Remember what 1 Corinthians 13 says about love, spelling out the threat of selfishness, and calling for love to be expressed in patience, kindness and trust. This is the love which soon learns to develop such openness in the marriage, such a readiness to see the funny side, and refusal to be too serious, such a determination not to react, or sulk or take off in a huff if one's partner makes a constructive suggestion or criticism, that it grows constantly richer and deeper. In the very facing of the differences it is strengthened. It flourishes on give and take.

Questions for discussion

'Give and take' necessitates knowing a lot about our partners, not only the things deep in our heart but also those that are apparently trivial.

1. After reading the examples in the chapter, list the different experiences which you both bring to the marriage. Is compromise going to be necessary? In what areas?
2. We all laugh at the 'lid on the toothpaste' issue, but think for a moment of any odd personal habits you have. Or maybe ask your partner to tell you what they are! Do they need to be adjusted so that conflict or irritation do not occur?
3. Although not perhaps the most exciting part of marriage, housekeeping and domestic chores have to be done. Who will do them in your household and on the basis of what criteria?
4. If one or both of you has had to make a major career change as a result of getting married or having children, how do you feel now? Do you feel valued and fulfilled? Can any improvements be made?

9. Money and Possessions

Statistics on marriage reveal that money is one of the biggest causes of marital problems. We have no way of knowing whether these statistics are right, but we are aware of many couples who have had great difficulties over money. So we need to examine the use of money and discuss how to prevent it becoming a cause of strife, and how to make it a benefit to you both.

True wealth

Money is neither good nor bad; in itself it is neutral. The song 'Money is the root of all evil' is a misquotation of the Authorised Version's rendering of 1 Timothy 6:10: 'For the *love* of money is the root of all evil.' (The NIV puts it, 'The love of money is a root of all kinds of evil.') This drastically alters the emphasis. Hebrews 13:5 refers to the love of money immediately after the verse on marriage being held in honour ('Keep your lives free from the love of money and be content with what you have') and goes on to point out the real values of life for a Christian: '. . . because God has said, "Never will I leave you; never will I forsake you."'

The juxtaposition of these two verses seems more than accidental. As an old rhyme put it: 'The loss of gold is much, the loss of health is more, but losing Christ is such a loss as no man can restore.' Our values are to spring from the overwhelming privilege of knowing Christ and being his and of sharing in the riches of his grace day by day. He shows us what really matters in life. Like the psalmist in Psalm 73 there may be times when we find ourselves jealous of the financial success and material prosperity of others, but if we will 'go into the sanctuary' we will get our perspective restored:

Riches are not necessary for a happy marriage.

Yet I am always with you; you hold me by my right hand. You guide me with your counsel, and afterwards you will take me into glory. Whom have I in heaven but you? And earth has nothing I desire besides you. My flesh and my heart may fail, but God is the strength of my heart and my portion for ever.

Some of the happiest and most fulfilled Christian couples we have known have not had much in material terms but they have been wonderful to know and their marriages are rich and lovely. Of course, we know others who have considerable material possessions and who live equally fulfilled lives. The common key is that none has *love* of money. They are all generous according to their means and also have a generosity of spirit, fulfilling the words of our Lord that, 'It is more blessed to give than to receive' (Acts 20:35).

From the earliest days of your marriage, if not before, you must establish your philosophy about money and possessions. This will often require the give and take we wrote about in the last chapter.

One of you may have come from a fairly affluent home, where money was never in short supply and material possessions or holidays were never hesitated over on grounds of cost. The other may have come from a family that had a hard time financially and materially, where surviving was the objective, entailing careful housekeeping, clothes bought sparingly and holidays on the cheap. A fairly stringent rather than an affluent upbringing can be a better preparation for marriage, unless, of course, you have realised at first hand the emptiness of the philosophy of 'spend, spend, spend'. But whatever your backgrounds, what is now to be your *joint* attitude and standard?

Bank accounts
Unless you prefer to keep clear of financial institutions, you must decide about bank or building society accounts. We hope you will have a joint account – your trust in one another should give you no hesitation over that. If you are both earning, then your salaries or wages will be pooled and put into this account. In addition, you may well have personal bank accounts. You need some private money that you can call your own or you never have the freedom to buy presents for birthdays, Christmas and anniversaries; and you will probably wish to be able to buy your own clothes and treat yourself to an occasional luxury or give to others if you should want to do so.

In some marriages, when only the husband is earning, this is never considered and a sum of money is 'allowed' by the husband for all the housekeeping and no more. That is neither right, nor fair, nor loving as it devalues the wife. If the wife is not earning, then she, as well as her husband, must have a thought-through allocation of personal money.

What system will you establish? In our own system a sum of money is transferred each month by standing order from our joint account to Myrtle's personal account for her own use and for the housekeeping: food and cleaning materials etc., though in our case, not gas and electricity. You will need to be quite clear as to what is included and what is not, so that no misunderstanding arises. Any personal gifts to Myrtle go into her account, too. It is all quite open. The amount transferred is readily adjustable, and the joint account is available to us both as well. Michael was previously in banking and so keeps the joint accounts up to date, with a separate column for his personal money. Myrtle took the trouble to learn how to keep her own accounts. There are absolutely no secrets.

Credit cards
You may not want credit cards at all, but if you do (and we find them immensely helpful in that we can pace our spending and settle the bill once a month) you will need to decide whether to have joint or separate cards, or both. If you have been in the habit of using the credit card freely on impulse, you will need to change your ways and, at first, a joint card may be unwise as there will be considerable friction if one partner keeps spending well beyond your joint means. Yet in most cases you will be prepared to use the card responsibly and carefully, so that it is always possible to face the monthly 'day of reckoning' without too many shudders! The advantage of using a credit card rather than cheques is that you do not have to watch the day-to-day balance in your bank account, but deal with the main demands on it just once a month.

Cashcards
You will already have discovered how the use of bank cashcards can be a trap. It is easy to forget that one has drawn cash that way, isn't it? The small payment slip can easily be lost. Although we both have cashcards, Myrtle has hers on her own account and Michael on the joint account, so that we can each keep our accounts up to date.

Payment of bills
If you are both earning you will need to work out who pays for what, how you share your joint resources and how much you retain separately. Marriages where the wife or husband keeps all she or he earns while expecting the partner to provide the money for housekeeping and the like are hardly operating in the oneness pledged on the wedding day.

Possessions
Similarly, you may each (or just one of you) come to marriage with considerable possessions or private income. At your wedding you pledge: 'All that I am I give you and all that I have I share with

you.' Think about how this will be worked out between you. Will you pool everything or keep a portion for yourself? If one of you retains huge personal spending power, it will not help the commitment of marriage – in fact, it denies the pledge you have made. If you really love each other you will freely share everything.

Debt

You must talk about how you will live according to your means. Debt is crippling. The vicious spiral of paying high interest rates and not cutting spending pushes many couples into deeper and deeper problems and despair. Although there are times when debt is necessary (for example, in hire purchase or a mortgage) this should be only for definite projects, with the repayment costs carefully calculated, along with the alternatives (such as waiting, rather than using hire purchase). Debt as a result of simply spending too much is foolish, careless and disastrous. Delaying the day of payment by playing one credit card against another is also a recipe for deep trouble. Inevitably this rebounds onto the marriage relationship, sometimes with mutual recrimination.

In some marriages there are times when one or the other reacts to tension by going out and spending, spending, spending. Sometimes the pressure of media advertising pushes us (especially through our children) into expenditure we cannot afford.

However, we hope *you* will be content with what you have – not envious of the neighbours – constantly relearning where true values are to be found.

Keeping accounts

Some married couples may operate safely and well by 'common sense' but, in order to control their money, most need to keep proper accounts. Those with accounting experience will set up their own system, but for those without such experience it is really important to learn the basics. Couples who go to the bank machine to find out what the balance in their bank account is are careless. Machines may not tell you of uncleared cheques and not everybody pays in their cheques at once. If you keep accounts up to date and check them against your monthly bank statement you will never need to 'ask the machine'. Accounts help you to plan

Christians know that giving is the first claim on their finances.

and keep to a budget for all your outgoing expenses. (See the two budget models at the end of this chapter.)

Giving
Think about your level of giving. If you are Christians you will know that giving is the first claim on your finances and not the last. You may decide to accept the Old Testament standard of giving a tenth of your income. Or you may resolve on a twentieth or less. If, from the start, your giving is proportionate to your income, a huge amount of money will be released for giving during the course of

your married life.

Should the percentage you give be before tax or after tax? Should it be after deduction for housing? You must decide. Our own custom is to write down in a separate column the amount we intend to use for giving. Once a month we draw out cash from it for offerings and the like; we draw cheques or standing orders on it for other giving. Special offerings, for building projects or other particular needs, usually have to come from our general savings.

Your main responsibility in giving is to your church, as only members of the church will give it support: we reckon about 50 per cent of the amount we have set aside. The rest will be for other causes, Christian and secular, which many more will support. Include missionary societies, world need and support for particular people or projects. Churches that have sensibly moved into pledged giving without passing collecting plates make it possible for you to give by standing order. Otherwise you have to keep cash in a drawer as 'tithing money' for either of you to use in services or to put in offertory envelopes.

Insurances

Immediately you are married you ought to take out some insurance policies, if you can afford to do so. Firstly, you need to insure your home and contents. Indeed, it is clearly better to do that *before* the wedding so that wedding gifts are covered. (By the way, it may be best to leave presents with a relative while you are on your honeymoon, as a wedding and the newly-weds' address are public knowledge and thieves may take advantage of your absence.)

Then you have the question of life assurance. Strangely, some Christians seem to think that life assurance is incompatible with trust in God. But it is an act of love and shows responsible care for one another. 1 Timothy 5:8 gives a strong biblical requirement to provide for relatives: 'If anyone does not provide for his relatives, and especially for his immediate family, he has denied the faith and is worse than an unbeliever.' If you have a home of your own on mortgage then you will have had to take out insurance. It is always best to take the form of insurance that makes the house entirely the partner's if either of you dies, to avoid leaving an enormous burden to carry alone in mortgage repayments. Insurance on your lives, redeemable at retirement or death, is necessary and wise if you can afford it. Extend insurance carefully as your circumstances allow, especially with reference to your children during school years.

A will

It sounds morbid but, again, it is a caring act to make a will. If the worst happened, it could mean fewer difficulties for your partner. It will need updating over the years, if you have a family, but make a will straightaway. At this stage it will usually be a simple bequeathing of your money and possessions to the other partner but you also need to designate beneficiaries in case you both die together, in an accident, for instance. Many churches and societies have been thankful for the thoughtfulness of people who name them among the beneficiaries.

Relax

Finally, if you set up accounts and keep your finances on an even keel, you can relax a little. We have found that often we have had to encourage one another to buy something – a new shirt, a new blouse – as it is possible to be over-stringent.

We also hope you will enjoy what you have rather than fret over what you do not have. Living within one's means may affect the standard of treats and outings, but you still need to have treats and enjoyable times out. In our first year of marriage, when we were living on a very small income, our weekly treat was a Crunchie bar each on our day off – and we enjoyed it enormously. Later it was cream cake and coffee at the Dairy Centre. Then we progressed to a meal or a film on special occasions.

If before your marriage you lived in a style of easy spending, if you always had wine for entertaining and could afford expensive holidays, you may find it difficult to cut back now to pay the mortgage. Look at it positively. What you took for granted will now become a treat. You will begin to value things more and have greater understanding of those who have never been well off or, in the hunger-ridden areas of the world, have nothing like even your present standard. Be thankful for what you do have; let money be your servant and even a friend (flexible or inflexible!), but never let it be your love.

Budget Model – 1

1. Draw up a budget for the year.

2. Divide into:

a. Regular monthly   £

food bills
_____

cash allowance for wife *and* husband
_____

cash for giving
_____

mortgage
_____

telephone/fuel/insurance etc.
_____

house and car maintenance
_____

b. Annual/one-offs etc.

clothes
_____

holidays
_____

annual bills
_____

covenanted giving
_____

Christmas
_____

replacement of major items (car, machines, etc.)
_____

savings
_____

3. Put the amount in (b) away by Standing Order into an interest-bearing account, with a cheque facility to pay credit card bills, etc.
And, in a multi-column cash book, tot up actual amounts spent in each category, with the budget shown at the top for comparison.

Budget Model – 2

1. Work out the annual costs for fuel (electricity, gas, etc.), telephone, water, local taxes, insurance premiums, mortgage repayments or rent, car, savings, standing order payments. Decide which to combine under different headings.

2. Divide each sum by 12 if you are on a monthly income, or by 52 if on weekly wages.

3. Each month or week transfer into each column the 12th or 52nd.

4. What is then left goes into your cash column and is your *only* available spending money for anything not in the budget.

5. See page 91 for an example of the cash book based on a monthly salary.

February/March

Date	Debit	Credit	Item	Cheque No.	Fuel Gas etc.	Car	Mortgage Insurance Standing Orders	Holidays	Savings	Giving	Clothes	Cash	Bank
Feb													
1		1,200.00	Salary		100.00	100.00	600.00	50.00	100.00	100.00	50.00	100.00	1,200.00
2	180.00		Stdg order: Wife				420.00						1,020.00
2	300.00		Stdg order: Mortgage				120.00						720.00
3	30.00		Cash for giving	001						70.00			690.00
3	20.00		Petrol	002		80.00							670.00
10	75.70		Gas bill	003	24.30								594.30
10	30.00		Cashpoint									70.00	564.30
18	25.00		Skirt	004							25.00		539.30
24	20.00		Outing to film & meal	005								50.00	519.30
March													
1		1,200.00	Salary		124.30	180.00	720.00	100.00	200.00	170.00	75.00	150.00	1,719.30
2	180.00		Stdg order: Wife				540.00						1,539.30
2	300.00		Stdg order: Mortgage				240.00						1,239.30
6	80.00		Car repairs	006		100.00							1,159.30
6	20.00		Petrol	007		80.00							1,139.30
8	70.00		Stdg order: insurance				170.00						1,069.30
10	177.00		Credit card bill	008									892.30
			DIY shop									112.00	
			Holiday deposit					30.00					
			Shirt & underwear								27.00		
			Kettle									91.00	892.30
10	50.00		Cashpoint									41.00	842.30
23	20.00		Petrol	009		60.00							822.30
23	150.00		Local taxes bill	010			20.00						672.30
23	30.00		Missionary society	011						140.00			642.30
23	50.00		Cash for giving							90.00			592.30
TOTAL	1,807.70	2,400.00	Balance at 31 March		124.30	60.00	20.00	30.00	200.00	90.00	27.00	41.00	592.30

Note: The sums used in these accounts are meant to illustrate only the principle.
Account Books with multiple columns are readily available: ours has 17 columns.

Questions for discussion

Money can be the cause of problems in a marriage. Have you considered how your financial situation will affect your relationship?

1. What do you think it means to love money? Do you recognise aspects of this in yourself?
2. Use the chapter as a check list. Consider each suggestion in detail, working out what the practical implications will be for you.

In the UK, we have the immense benefit of giving by covenant and thus greatly increasing the value of the gift, as the church or charity can get the value of the tax refunded. This is a highly responsible way of giving. Gift Aid is now possible too, for block gifts over £400, and here the tax is reclaimable at once. Many Christians in the UK use the Charities Aid Foundation as agent for their giving, the tax value being handled by them and cheques making giving simple.

10. Children

Childbirth is a moment of overwhelming joy and emotion. We have seen numbers of men and women come to faith in Christ as a result of the birth of their first child. And even those without faith have spoken to us of being on a 'spiritual high' at the birth, especially fathers, when they have been able to be present. Whatever the pain and difficulty prior to the birth, the joy of seeing this precious new life, fruit of your union, part of you both, is deeply moving. You have shared together in the creativity of God and, like the psalmist, can say, 'Children are a heritage from the Lord and the fruit of the womb is his gift' (Psalm 127:4, ASB version). In those early moments of dream-like joy, give thanks to God together and dedicate your new parenthood and your new baby to his love.

You will never be the same again! Your life will never be the same again! You are now a family and not just a couple. Your baby will make demands day and night, and you may wonder whether you will ever again have a peaceful night's sleep. You will! What is important is to keep an 'over-ride' of thankfulness for this precious gift and positively enjoy every rapidly changing stage of your child's and, later, children's development.

You will have an enormous sense of joy at the first smile, the first responses of unintelligible 'words', the first teeth, the starting to crawl and so on. Your wonder and thankfulness will not diminish. It goes on into the excitement of starting nursery school and through all the stages of school life, on to leaving school, further training, work, and perhaps marriage and then your first grandchildren. It is non-stop, but enriching, stretching, rewarding and great fun. You both need to share in it all – and that includes fathers changing nappies!

The need for security

Your children's greatest need is you and your love together. You can give them no better help than your commitment to each other, your obvious love for one another, your fulfilled and positive lifestyle, your shared faith in Christ and the security of your home. No amount of teaching, disciplining or generosity can make up for a faulty parental relationship. What you are together is seen, experienced and often copied – for better or for worse. Therefore the centre of the family must always be the marriage, not the child. If children are the hub of the marriage wheel, there is often a collapse of the marriage when children leave home. Nevertheless, although your children must not be the centre, they must never doubt your love for them and their high value in your attitude and thinking.

Standards, limits and love

A primary tension is that of discipline. Parental policies range from never disciplining a child through to insisting on a very strict upbringing. Proverbs 22:6 says, 'Train a child in the way he should go, and when he is old he will not turn from it.' Proverbs 23:13 adds, 'Do not withhold discipline from a child.'

We still need to apply these principles, but the world of today is very different from the world as the writer of Proverbs knew it. In the first place, there is a huge influence from outside the home. When Proverbs was written, the family, the wider family and the nation would have shared many of the same principles. But we live in a country where, though much of our legislation and many of our institutions have Christian roots, the prevailing culture is far from Christian. The insidious influence of popular culture on young people, backed by peer pressure, can flood the stream in which we have guided our children and sadly can often burst the banks and change the course.

All this is a long way on from your wedding day, but it should affect your thinking about discipline from the earliest days. The children who are too severely disciplined and prevented from sharing at least the neutral aspects of their peer group (clothing styles, music, choice of bedroom colour and so on) are the most likely to rebel when they can. Although each teenager must become his or her own person, this need not involve a radical rejection of the

Your children's greatest need is you and your love together.

parents' standards if there has been at least as much love as discipline.

So do you discipline? Yes, we have no doubt about that as a principle, for children have a sinful bias from the beginning (it is one of the surprises to see this wilfulness showing itself in your tiny baby!). If that bias towards entire self-centredness is allowed free rein there will grow up a very selfish person, family life will become almost intolerable and the parents' marriage will be pushed off-centre. Actually, an undisciplined child is far more unhappy than the gently disciplined child, because the lack of limits breeds insecurity.

The key, of course, is to exercise discipline only when you can match it with the assurance of love. In Ephesians 6:1–4 children are told to obey their parents 'in the Lord' and to honour their father and mother. But then fathers are told, 'Do not exasperate your children.' For we are also sinners with a bias towards self and, therefore, have to try and ensure that disciplining is not for our self-interest and our peace and quiet. Children do, of course, need to learn consideration for other members of the family, but we also need to show consideration for them as part of the family. For instance, a fatherly remonstrance, too strongly expressed because of personal tiredness, is wrong and damaging, failing in love and respect for the child as a human being.

A Christian home

It may well be that you will have standards in your household that differ from some of your neighbours, usually because you are seeking to live as a Christian family. The gentle working through of Christian principles with your growing children will need to be matched by love in action. For instance, you will have a distinctive way of handling Sunday. Worshipping together will be primary (and we deal with this in the next chapter) but there may also be things you do not consider right to do on a Sunday. If that is so, you need to be positively creative in your alternatives, making them better than the activities that are 'not done'.

Make the day special. Let the food always be the best of the week with, for instance, a tradition of a choice of sweet to which a 'yes – please' is the recognised request for them all! Part of the day could be spent going out together or playing board games or encouraging hobbies. The aim must always be to make the day a happy day as you worship and share activities and pleasures together.

Even if all the material luxuries are not possible, your home should be a fun place which all the family enjoy and to which no member hesitates to bring friends. The principle of outmatching any necessary negatives by creative positives has many applications. Limitation of money may mean simpler holidays than the expensive package holidays of your neighbours, but there is no reason at all why you cannot on a small budget provide a far 'better' holiday in terms of family enjoyment. It will involve thought, time and imagination and though it may not be much of a rest for you as parents, it will be a great family time. These are lovely years that will soon slip by and they are worth working at.

Money

Money can cause headaches. It is not easy for a child if friends at school can always have the latest gadget, up-to-date fashion clothes and a large allowance for pocket money (our lads knew a boy at their school who received a Porsche on his seventeenth birthday!). Clergy families such as ours feel the pressure, especially in teenage years, when a pair of the latest sports shoes or any clothing costs a great deal and youngsters want to keep up with the latest fashion trend.

You cannot spend what you cannot afford, or your children will push you into the debt spiral. The young children in the supermarket crying because they cannot have something they want may often use a version of the blackmail phrase: 'If you don't let me have it, you don't love me,' and the teenager may secretly feel the same unless the whole question of family finances is openly discussed.

One way out may be to give a clothing allowance to each teenager and let them decide on priorities. After learning the hard way that money is not elastic they will usually become more responsible. Yet again, it is important that you constantly reaffirm your love and show that you value them as people. Teaching them to live more simply, to live within their means, can in the end be a help to them for life. The headmaster of a boys' junior school said at a parents' day that the most fulfilled boys in the school were the children of the manse as they could not have everything they wanted and thus learnt the greater values of life. If it is true that your children can see your love for each other, your love for them, plus the love, joy, fun and fulfilment of family life, then they will gradually see that these are more important than material plenty.

Leisure and free time

Time together as a family is essential in the formative years. When fathers (or fathers and mothers) work long hours, going off to work before the family is up and coming home when they are in bed, you need to think about how you can do things together at the weekends and holidays. There will come a time when the growing youngster does not necessarily want to be part of the family for leisure activities, of course, but even then it is good to *try* to do some things together.

The demands of life in the ministry meant our putting considerable emphasis on holidays and short breaks. One of the best decisions we ever made was to purchase a vehicle in which we could all five ride, eat and sleep. It became part of the family for fourteen years. Short breaks away, and adventurous holidays around the continent of Europe, carrying nearly all our food so that it was 'on the cheap', were some of the happiest times of our family togetherness. The fun of parking on a beach in Sweden, with a late-night swim, and an early-morning swim as well for those who wanted it, the ferries, the border posts, the foreign languages and the shopping, the cable cars and the walks were enjoyed by us all. Even now we are all quite nostalgic about those years! They were formative and deepening times in our family life which bear their full fruition in our relationship together now, with all three of our grown up and married children and their spouses. Be creative and fun families – according to your means.

Sharing your love

It will be part of your Christian life to serve others and to share your home. We talk about this more fully in a later chapter, but raise it here because it affects your family. We would suggest a sensitive adaptability as your children grow up. Ours thoroughly enjoyed an open home in their early years. Various people lived with us at different times, some working in the area, some students and others who were in need of help. This was an asset to family life while our children were small. Then there were the meetings we held in our house, and the Sunday tea-parties, often with thirty or more present and the children helping to serve the food.

In the teenage years, adjustments were necessary. This was more often the time when our youngsters brought their friends into the home and big open teas were not helpful to family life. Later we came to the stage when our children were co-leading or co-organising events in the home and the wheel had gone full circle. We learnt together the value of Christian witness through the use of the home.

Another aspect of family life is your service together outside the home. Early Christmases were great family and fun times in different relatives' homes, but in London there was a tradition of providing Christmas Day lunch at the church for all who would otherwise be alone. As a family we all agreed to having presents after supper on Christmas Eve so that on Christmas Day we could share in the running of the lunch and the entertainment after it, plus transporting people home. The family celebrations then continued on Boxing Day.

We also all had tasks in the church – each of our three children being involved in the music or with the television/audio team. In serving we drew together as a team, as well as a family.

In the sight of God

One of our friends helped us when he said how he had suddenly realised the minimal difference of a mere twenty-five years between himself and his children when he thought in eternal terms. We are *all* precious to our Lord in our own right. The relationship of parent to child fades into equality before our Lord. We are equally sinners; we can be equally his children for ever. You will not have brought merely a child into the world – nor only a potential adult – but a person who can live eternally! A constant awareness of this affects your praying and spiritual encouragement, but it also influences your growing sense of friendship and fellowship, so that you learn from one another, and strengthen, help and encourage one another. We have increasingly received help and encouragement, as well as information, from our adult family and their splendid spouses.

In the even wider sense we have to see that the family of Christ is more important than our own human relationship. 'Here are my mother and my brothers,' said Christ, pointing to his disciples, when he was challenged to confine himself to the wishes of his human family (Mark 3:31–5). Our family life should not act as a restraint on this wider dimension.

Talking together

Openness is vital in good family life. If possible, seek to achieve an atmosphere in your home in which your growing children feel free to share anything and everything. It will require your developing a listening ear and a generous spirit. An immediate negative reaction to something you are being told will stem the flow at that moment and in the future. Often the important sharing comes when you are busy preparing a meal in the kitchen or late at night when you are exhausted and your youngsters are really waking up! If you have to say 'another time', fix that time there and then. Do not just put it off indefinitely.

Many young people never have any serious conversations with an adult in or out of the home. Although this is particularly true in less literate or less educated families, it can also be true in the homes of powerful executives who are 'too busy' to talk.

Walking, sailing, shopping, a football match, a tennis tournament, a game of golf or a visit to a place of interest – father and son, mother and daughter, father and daughter, mother and son – two by two – these are important opportunities for sharing, conversation and opening the heart. They will not happen without planning and must be regarded as unalterable engagements in your diary. The busy parent must say to others: 'I am booked on that day.' The danger, for instance, in clergy families of everyone but the family getting father's time has to be avoided. A balance must be struck.

When our family was small, we had our day off in the middle of the week, but moved to Saturdays when they were teenagers as this was a far better day for flexibility, even with weddings. Usually on Saturday evenings we relaxed in the family lounge, whether all members of the family were at home or not.

Another major place for sharing and conversation is the meal-table, and a balance needs to be struck between having the television on during meals because of a programme most want to watch, and having it off so that you can enjoy the time together. Video recorders are liberating in this respect.

'Well done!'

Encouragement is always more helpful than criticism. We all need encouragement whoever we are and whatever our age. In particular, your children will thrive on your interest and your boosting of them in their school-work, their hobbies, their sport, their achievements and even their friendships.

Myrtle did much more of this in our family. The draining demands of church responsibility meant that most of Michael's evenings were given over to activities and Myrtle went alone to most prize-givings, parents' evenings, concerts, and speech days. She gave most of the encouragement, and offered the listening ear and the gentle words of guidance (Michael is writing this bit!). Although give and take is necessary, we were a little off-balance in this sphere. Try yourselves to give as much *joint* encouragement as you can.

One area of encouragement that needs discernment is over each child's development. Just as one baby may be 'easy', sleeping at night and so on, and the next 'difficult' in not sleeping and in crying a lot, so each child has different gifts, abilities, talents and character. The last thing you must do is force them into the same

Openness is vital in good family life.

mould – into your own mould – about achievements and career. Your aim should be to enable every child to be fulfilled in accordance with that child's special talents and abilities, and never to think of one as superior or inferior by some academic or other standard.

There will similarly be variations in sporting and leisure interests. The parents who spend most of their leisure time sailing, for instance, may produce a sailing-mad family, but if one or more children are not interested, there must be no pressure to conform, but encouragement to develop in a different sphere. The accusation that 'bringing up a child in practice is more like bringing down a person' need never be true in a good family.

Godparents

As a family we have all valued the support of friends (as well as relatives, of course) who have come alongside us. Godparents have been invaluable, so much so that some younger relatives in a Baptist church, who have seen how important godparents have been to our three children, are inventing equivalents! Carefully chosen, they can become real friends to their godchild – in prayer, in giving, but especially in encouragement. In particular, youngsters can often share things with a godparent (or a relative) that they might find difficult to talk about at home.

We are also thankful for other friends who have become 'aunts' and 'uncles' to our children. Mutual benefit is gained. They also are often wise givers of advice when required (but are rapidly dropped by youngsters if they give advice when it is not required!).

The spiritual care and responsibility you must exercise are something we consider in the next chapter, but all we have said about encouragement, adaptation and sensitivity also applies to that vital area of upbringing.

The good times, and the bad

Enjoy your children to the full! The stages of development are rapid, and as other children come and the family grows older the dynamics of the family change continually. Do not let bringing up a family be a burden, even if it is demanding. Delight in it all, stage by stage. Face each new challenge creatively and prayerfully. Go on learning all the time how to be better parents.

Never hesitate to say 'sorry' to your children when you have acted or reacted wrongly or unfairly. One fatherly failure was when our daughter, during a post-Easter break in a cottage, brilliantly achieved the changing of every clock forward by an hour for April Fool's Day morning. This father remembers with pain how, instead of roaring with laughter, congratulating the achiever and enjoying it all, he reacted with sheer annoyance at being got up an hour early on holiday. Nor was 'sorry' readily forthcoming! Ah well! We live and learn – until the next time!

We have not talked about the problems of rebellion, when teenagers separate off from the family and take up anti-Christian stances on moral or theological issues. We empathise deeply with the pain of those friends who through no fault in their parenthood have had to experience this. A discussion on teenage rebellion and problems needs a whole book and anything we can say here will be inadequate. Suffice it to say (as our wounded friends would also say) that love has to be maintained as far as possible.

The story of the Prodigal Son does not tell us that any attempt was made to bring the son back, since what he had done was deliberate and decisive. (In contrast, the accidental loss of the sheep and the coin necessitated going out to search [Luke 15].) Instead, the father waited, looked, longed and at the first indication of a turning back, ran to meet his son, bringing about a wonderful restoration. Our love, longing and constant prayer may be all that we can do. Words, letters and remonstrations are usually better left aside or they may further harden the already hardening heart. These are sensitive, deep and painful matters and parents going through such times need much support, encouragement and love. A helpful book on this is *Parents in Pain* by John White (IVP).

However, at this stage of your life, as you are entering marriage, lift up your eyes to the positive, creative and enriching years ahead. Think with hope and with the best expectations. Your problems will only be 'little ones'. So we hope with all our heart that you will have a family – either children physically born to you or adopted (both are equally precious). We hope you will have a marvellous family life and know the joy of seeing your family grow up – and perhaps marry – and then thrill you with grandchildren (they are great!). Children will delight, annoy, captivate, frustrate and make you laugh and cry – but always love them, and enjoy them!

Questions for discussion

In this chapter we read that 'childbirth is a moment of overwhelming joy and emotion' – but are we ready? However, there is a danger of never being ready, never being in the right house, never having the right salary, etc.

1. Consider together when it would be the right time to start trying for a family. On what basis are you making this decision?
2. Reflect back on your own childhood. How was discipline exercised? Do you think this would be the right way to discipline your own children?
3. Have you any good ideas about making family time a special time? Perhaps you know families who do interesting activities or have special traditions that you could replicate? Are there traditions that you would like to carry on from your own childhood?
4. How will you ensure that you review the use of your home and remain ready to adapt as family circumstances change across the years?

11. God-Centredness

God at the centre

The wedding service is permeated with God-centredness. God's love is the overriding theme. As we have seen, the exhortation in the wedding service refers both to the basis of marriage as part of God's purposes in creation and to Christ's self-giving love for the church as the pattern for marital love. Your vows are taken 'in the name of God'; you promise to live and love together 'according to God's law'; you give each other your bodies and all you possess 'within the love of God, Father, Son and Holy Spirit'; you are declared to be man and wife 'in the presence of God'; and, when your hands are joined, the words are: 'What God has joined together. . .'.

The prayers relate to your love for each other, continuing in God's love and being blessed with the riches of his grace. They ask that you may please God in your lives together with a faithfulness in your commitment to each other, and that he may give you wisdom, strength and comfort in your companionship. God is asked to enable you to be good witnesses to his love, to bless your home and your child-bearing and to help you to be effective agents of his love in a troubled world. God is so much more important in the wedding service than worries about rings, hands, vows and clothes!

Christian marriage is in the context of God's love, it is inspired by God's love and is to breathe God's love. There is no suggestion in the wedding service that the church is an addendum or that God is an optional extra.

Christian marriage embraces every aspect of life. Nothing is outside the enlightening and strengthening grace of God. Your standards, your aims, your use of time and money, your serving of others, your reading, your television viewing, your possessions, the way you face sickness or trouble – everything is in the glorious enfolding of your whole being in Christ as part of his family. The whole of your life is worship, a worship which is expressed in everyday living but is focused in services or other acts of worship.

Facing up to God

It may be that the theme of this chapter makes you feel ill at ease. Perhaps your contact with the church is fairly nominal or distant. You are not against the faith, you think you believe and you want God's blessing on your marriage, but you are not really committed to Christ and the church.

We want the very best for you, and so urge you to be like many other couples we have known, just like you, who have faced up to God and the reality of faith in Christ together as they approached marriage. In Michael's years as a bishop it has been a frequent privilege to confirm couples in the faith who have talked through the Christian truth with their minister because they wanted to enter fully into the meaning of the wedding service. They have come to a living faith, and their marriage has been a wonderful new start in more ways than one – they have begun married life and the Christian life at the same time.

Do face up to this, the most important issue for every human being. If one of you has a living faith and the other has not, may we gently urge the one without to swallow pride and go off alone to see your minister? Begin your marriage as you mean to go on – with God not at the circumference but in the centre.

Moving forward

'Heirs together of the grace of life' is how the apostle Peter (1 Peter 3:7, AV) speaks of a Christian couple in marriage. Stated baldly like that, the words are a little out of context. If you look at the whole passage you will see that consideration and respect are basic attitudes 'so that nothing will hinder your prayers' and thus impede the flow of grace. In other words, the ongoing blessing on a marriage, its growth in love, and its spiritual depth and maturity, do not happen automatically. Your attitudes to one another and your looking directly to God in prayer and worship are vital for that grace to flow. You will recall that in Ephesians 5 the call to 'submit to one another' is 'out of reverence for Christ'.

If you are Christians, you will already have a rhythm of worship and, hopefully, of personal prayer and Bible reading. You will also probably be a member of a fellowship group, and be involved in several aspects of the church's life and witness. Now you come together. New demands will be made on the timetable of daily life. When you have a family, the impact on your personal time can be catastrophic! In principle, you will want to maintain your devotional growth. If you keep that purpose constantly clear before you, rather like a compass point, you will not neglect to make the frequent adjustments necessary in order to remain close to God in the changing circumstances of life.

Personal prayer times

First, think about how you will share spiritually as a couple. We hope you will establish the unfailing habit of taking it in turns to pray briefly at the end of the day – God will not mind if you are in bed at the time! Long drawn-out prayers at that point, or even *both* praying each night, do not, in our experience, fit the moment.

Some couples start their day with Bible reading, prayer and worship together (some use the morning service in the *Book of Common Prayer* or the *Alternative Service Book*). This can be difficult when children are small, or if one partner cannot wake up in the mornings! However, many couples find this the best way throughout the whole of their married life.

We have always preferred to read, pray and worship separately on most mornings. We each find meditation easier when we are on our own, following our own thinking and patterns of prayer (we have different systems which suit us individually). It is also easier for us as we prefer different times. Myrtle will spend her time alone with God before or after breakfast, or later on, according to the demands of a particular day. Michael normally needs to have this time before breakfast. What we have found particularly useful is both keeping to the same pattern of daily Bible reading so that later in the day we can share the help we have received from it.

Your pattern of life will no doubt be very different from ours, if at first you are both rushing off to work by bus, train or car. Some still secure the early time, achieving it by sheer discipline, not least over when they go to bed at night. Others adapt to reading and praying on public transport, or arrive at work early enough to find a quiet spot, or use tapes in the car. Mothers at home use times when little ones are having a sleep or have all gone off to school. The adaptations will be manifold, but the principle is vital. Your personal spiritual health depends on devotion, on being fed by Scripture and on praying for others.

Worshipping together
Your focus of worship will, of course, be on Sundays, and perhaps mid-week services or meetings. There is something very special about worshipping together at the start of your marriage – and this has continued to be a great joy to us all through our married life, even though we are usually in different parts of the church (so we especially value the opportunities to sit together on holiday). Your coming to worship without rush, in a spirit of prayer for the service, and of openness to God, and your readiness to share the good things you received later in it, adds to your growth and joy. So does your reading of Christian books as well as your training together in Christian understanding and for practical service.

Praying together
Special prayers – sometimes emergency 'telegram' prayers – will be a natural part of your life for yourselves and for others. In our first three years of marriage Myrtle had to go into hospital seven times, and this stimulated a frequent sharing in prayer – which on several occasions finished with the approaching sound of the ambulance siren.

Joys as well as needs ought to be shared quite naturally in prayer. Some dramatic incidents, as when one of our youngsters was rushed into hospital with suspected meningitis, have thrown us to our knees.

It may be that you will have to face some special problem or illness during marriage. How far, for instance, do you pray for healing? We have had to face both chronic and sudden illness together and in the light of 2 Corinthians 12:8–9 we brought each situation to God. Sometimes his purpose for us, with the skill of doctors, was healing, and at other times we came to accept that verse 9:

'My grace is sufficient for you' was to be the way. We believe it right to pray for God's glory to be revealed and known and to rejoice whether that comes through healing or in grace to cope.

In later years we also developed the habit of 'extended grace' at meals. We have always had 'grace', but kept it brief while the family was young. As the children became young people and increasingly shared the faith for themselves, extended graces became possible. This simply means adding a few specific and immediately relevant thanksgivings or requests, arising from the activities of that day, or perhaps from a major news item or the needs of others (such as a friend having an operation at that time).

Praying with young children

If you are blessed with children, you will long for them to grow up into Christ. It is good to be praying all the way through the pregnancy (and before it!) and afterwards, of course, daily over and for the child. In the Old Testament God established covenants (agreements) between himself and his people. One of the fundamental covenants was with Abraham. In response to Abraham's faith, God promised to make Abraham the father of a family as numerous as the grains of sand on the seashore. Abraham received the sign of the covenant – circumcision – and then gave the sign to all male children born in his family. All children descended from Abraham received this sign. They were born into a covenant family. As Christians, we enter this same relationship of trust with God, through Christ. We share in the new covenant made by his death on the cross, and our 'circumcision' is spiritual, not physical. Our children, like Abraham's, are born into a covenant family, and join with us on the Christian pilgrimage. You will want to say publicly to God and the church that this is a child of a Christian family and will plan for baptism or (if you are a member of a Free Church) for dedication.

Myrtle carried the evening prayer times with our children, as clerical responsibilities left Michael with few free evenings. ('She was also very good at it,' adds Michael.) Praying over the cot later moved to praying with the children, in simple ways that they could understand. This led on to their suggesting (often with moving insight and love) subjects for prayer, or joining in. Nightly reading of a Bible story, often with an activity, continued until they were ready to take over praying and reading for themselves. At bedtime there were other stories, too, and it was a special time for cuddles and the quiet security of family love.

We did not go in for family prayers at the breakfast table, mainly because of some bad experiences in other homes, where it created tension because of buses to catch and problems of over-sleeping. But breakfast-time prayers do work well in some families. You may hear Christians speak as if you are failing should you not have family prayers. Do not let others hustle you. Do what is best for *your* family. Later, as our youngsters matured in their faith and Christian life, it was natural for us to pray more together – but extended grace was the normal method.

Children and church

Going to church together as a family will be part of life's normal pattern when your children are young. We hope you will see this continue when they are older. Sensitivity, tact, explanation and sharing may often be called for, but compulsion will usually be counter-productive. A strong sense of family unity can often help a teenager when peer pressure says that going to church is not for young people. Churches that have a lively and imaginative, out-of-the-rut and innovative youth work are invaluable at this stage!

What proved to be of the greatest value to all three of our children in their teenage years was participation in Christian house-parties and camps. It was here that they really grew and found their feet as Christians. The fellowship of other young Christians and the support of the leaders gave a boost like no other. These events give the opportunity to enjoy the freedom and sheer fun of being Christians together – and provide a lot of time to ponder Christian truth and its application to living as a Christian in the modern world.

Major Christian youth organisations also provide a splendid framework for support and growth both through large gatherings in big centres with modern music and expert presentation, and by magazines, literature and training programmes. Like many parents, we are thankful to God for this help as our children grew from youth into adulthood and into a full sharing in the faith and the church, in worship and leadership.

'All things richly to enjoy'

Some Christian homes are very stifling – and the children do not experience God-centredness so much as God-restrictiveness. The negatives loom larger than the positives. Even fairly harmless preferences in clothing, colours and music are bridled. Underneath the forced conformity simmers a rebellion which may erupt not only into a rebellious life-style as soon as school is left behind, but into a reaction against God. A God-centred home should be much more positive than negative. There must be some rules and standards, but the home ought to be a place of love, fun and encouragement – with a lot of laughter. Separate talents, tastes and styles need to be lived with, as far as they do not conflict with the priority of Christ.

When God is at the centre, we will be more open to promote the good things he has given us that are positive and creative. We are, says Paul, to give priority to the true, the noble, the right, the pure and to whatever is lovely, admirable, excellent and praiseworthy (Philippians 4:8). Appreciation of, and participation in, the arts and sciences, in music, and exploring the wonders of the natural creation, are fostered in a God-centred home. Sport belongs, too, as long as it does not become so consuming as to be an idol (and that can be true of any hobby). As a family we have particularly enjoyed our holidays when we have gone to mountainous areas. All our family have musical ability, and some have artistic talents in photography and painting. In Christ we see the world in a new light – the love of beauty is fired with deeper meaning; longing for the right and good is anchored to God's character; music does not just move the heart but stimulates praise and worship. God takes the best and makes it better.

Above all, this is true of love itself. God is love. We know him by love. His Spirit pours his love into our hearts. As the years pass, we know more and more of the height, depth, width and length of the love of God. So, a God-centred home should increasingly be a place of love and a God-centred marriage, a marriage of deepening love. Christ turns the water into wine! In fact, because you are in him who is love, you should be the greatest lovers in the world!

The text that emerged as specially 'ours' at the start of our marriage was this: 'Rejoice in the Lord alway: and again I say, Rejoice' (Philippians 4:4, AV). As Dr William Barclay interprets it: 'I know what I am saying. I've thought of everything that can possibly happen. And still I say – rejoice!' In those early years of illness and miscarriages we held on to this verse. It burnt into our hearts and faith. Its consequences (in the following verses) are that we commit everything to God in prayer and trust him to bring about his perfect will. This gives peace instead of worry and challenges the frustration we feel when we don't get what *we* want.

Several times we had to move to a parish in another part of Britain at strategic points in our children's schooling. This meant that we had to entrust our children and their development to God's grace. It was not easy for them or us – but the outcome has always evidently been over-ruled by God's care for them – even at the very last minute.

This is how it has been with all the varied decisions and quandaries we have had to face. We have prayed, trusted and had peace (more at some times than at others – we admit!). Yet the bottom line was always, 'Rejoice in the Lord always.' This puts God right at the centre – every day – every year – always! May he always be at the centre of our marriage and yours!

Questions for discussion

Reference to God cannot be avoided in the wedding service and his desire is for us to allow him to be Lord of our marriage as well.

1. 'Your personal spiritual health depends on devotion, on being fed by Scripture and on praying for others.' If you believe this to be the case, discuss how you are going to enable it to happen in your marriage. How will you remind each other of its vital importance and review progress? What are you both doing at the moment to strengthen your relationship with God?
2. How will you incorporate prayer into your daily lives?
3. If you are considering having a family or already have one, how will you communicate Christ to them? If you are from a Christian home, are there aspects of your upbringing that you would like to adapt to your own situation to help you to do this?

12. Service for Others

True love flows in several directions. It is poured into our hearts by the Holy Spirit, and we respond with love towards God. We love because he first loved us. Love should flourish and grow from each to the other in the marital relationship and should embrace our children. Yet it also needs to flow outwards in friendship, care, service and concern well beyond the boundaries of home and family. 'Streams of living water will flow from within' (John 7:38), is how our Lord described the outflow of the Spirit from a Christian. This will have been so in your single Christian lives. Christian marriage should double the flow!

If a marriage is caught up in itself, looking inwards, concerned almost totally with its own welfare, prosperity and interests, it becomes more of a Dead Sea than a flowing stream. Indeed, some would describe such selfish love as idolatry. It is certainly a sad reflection of the Christian faith if it occurs in Christians and is as disgraceful as when the Priest and Levite in the parable of the Good Samaritan failed their God by self-interest, ignoring the wounded traveller on the Jericho Road. Christ told us that those who live for themselves lose themselves, and that those who give themselves for others find themselves (Mark 8:34–5). The same is true in marriage. The self-centred marriage and family go sour; the self-giving family is fresh and attractive, and, since love is seldom just one way, is constantly refreshed by the response of those it helps.

Loving and serving

A husband and wife in a love-match marriage with outgoing love are often unaware that they are serving others, because serving is a normal part of their attitude to living. You may recall that in the parable of the Sheep and the Goats in Matthew 25 those who are called 'the righteous' respond with surprise: 'Lord, when did we see you hungry and feed you, or thirsty and give you something to drink? And when did we see you a stranger and invite you in, or needing clothes and clothe you? When did we see you sick or in prison and go to visit you?' (Matthew 25:37–9). Their care for those in need was part of their normal living – and our Lord said that this care was shown to him.

Similarly, in his first letter, John says, 'If anyone has material possessions and sees his brother in need but has no pity on him, how can the love of God be in him?' (1 John 3:17). To put this the other way round, if God's love is part of us, then doing what we can about the needs of others will be a 'natural' part of our life. We rightly react against 'do-gooders' because they usually press their do-gooding on others more to satisfy their own conscience than to help other people, and their do-gooding is unrelated to the rest of their life. Doing good should rather be so interwoven in the fabric of our life that love to God, marital love and love to others is a matching and blending whole.

Paul's friends

Aquila and Priscilla

Aquila and Priscilla (whom we meet in Acts 18:1–4, 18–28) are a good example of a loving and serving couple. They had to set down their roots lightly, moving from Italy to Corinth, later to Syria and then on to Ephesus with Paul. This flexibility was far easier without children (at least, there is no mention of children) and, wherever they were, it seems their home was open. They welcomed Paul when he came to Corinth, and he stayed in their home for eighteen months, joining with them at their trade of tent-making. They gave time to individuals, explaining the faith carefully to Apollos.

They encouraged others, and took the trouble to write a letter of support for Apollos. They 'risked their lives', says Paul, in the service of Christ, and he adds, 'Not only I but all the churches of the Gentiles are grateful to them' (Romans 16:3–4).

Their pioneering work with the gospel led them to begin the church in their home (Romans 16:5 and 1 Corinthians 16:19). You feel the warmth of their 'hearty greetings in the Lord' (1 Corinthians 16:19, RSV) – nothing cool about their love!

As we read about Priscilla and Aquila we feel they are the sort of people we would have liked to know. They would have been lovely friends with a home that would not always have been tidy, nor yet recovered from the last move, but open, relaxed and friendly, in which people mattered more than things.

Children growing up in such an atmosphere will unconsciously imbibe it so that it moulds their own approach to life. Then they will naturally turn outwards to others in care and service instead of being consumed by self-interest, material possessions, their own pleasure and comfort. If your home has the marks of Aquila and Priscilla's, it will be a blessing to many. Blessed too will be your children – and others will be blessed by their lives.

Friends and neighbours

'Who is my neighbour?' the lawyer asked Jesus, because 'he wanted to justify himself' (Luke 10:29). The parable of the Good Samaritan was our Lord's response. Neighbourliness obviously starts with those across the garden fence or the back wall. We have been thankful to God for individuals and couples in parishes where we have served who have been known in their street or place of work as the people to whom you turn with a problem or need. Equally, we have been saddened when the accusation is made that Christians live only for themselves or for pressing others to go to church, but are never ready to help or give a hand when needs arise, be it in the street or the office.

The story is told that when Thomas Jefferson was President of the United States, he and others with him came on horseback to a flooded river. Together they considered whether or not to cross it. Along the bank were people without horses, hoping to get across. One of them came up to Jefferson and asked whether he could ride with him. Jefferson readily agreed, and they forded the river successfully. On the other side the man was asked whether he chose that rider because he was the president. The man replied that he had not known he was the president; the reason he had approached him was because he had a 'yes' face. Christian marriages, flowing in and with God's love, should have a 'yes' face, not a 'no' face.

Neighbourliness goes further, of course. It includes those we meet at the clinic, the nursery school, fellow parents at school events, colleagues at work, those we have contact with in shopping, sports activities, evening classes and so on. It is expressed particularly in the church fellowship as we welcome the stranger, come alongside the needy and befriend the lonely.

Sometimes couples reluctantly make the decision that it is hopeless trying to be members of their local church, perhaps because of the preaching (or lack of it), or a doctrinal oddity or failure to provide for children. Some do manage to keep going and gradually help the church to change. Some give up and attend a church in another town or area. Others keep local in the morning and go for a spiritual 'tonic' elsewhere in the evening!

We mention this here because service and involvement in your local community will require deliberate effort if you are members of a church elsewhere. When you are part of the local church you are more easily also part of the community. Interest in the local area, its amenities, activities, schools and social needs has to be part of our neighbourly thinking, rather than being 'passed by on the other side' as we go off to church elsewhere.

Christian couples can have a considerable influence in a local area, not least because they do not give up easily but try to see causes and enterprises through to fruition.

The world out there

These days neighbourliness is worldwide. Needs and challenges bombard us from all parts of the world through the media. We cannot possibly respond to every need, just as we cannot support every good cause that sends its requests through our letter box. We have to be selective in the giving of money and support. Yet the needs of the world must always be in front of us. For some this has meant an uprooting, children and all, to settle in another part of the country or world. It has involved giving up good jobs and a comfortable life-style. Some couples have done this after early retirement and when the family has grown up.

Young people can experience the needs of the Third World by going out on work projects or in service to an overseas church. Parental investment in the costs of this are well rewarded by the added dimension to family life and attitudes. There are opportunities for service in this country too, for a year after leaving school or university, or in vacations, helping to run camps, house-parties or missions. Some may want to go full time into pastoral ministry or social service. In a loving Christian home, where service to others is natural and spontaneous, a young person's wish to serve the wider world community is not restrained by ambition and parental pressure to get on and get established in life.

Serving others can be somewhat sanitised if it keeps to the more pleasant arenas. Conscience is satisfied because it is service, but areas of the country, aspects of society, parts of the world that are not in line with our background, or where we feel 'uncomfortable', or which offend our taste are quietly avoided. Reasons can always be found if we are challenged. The couple who ask God *where* they should live may find themselves going to an area where there are few Christians and where talented help in the local church will be invaluable, rather than to a 'nice' area with a 'very nice' church and a surfeit of talented people.

It is said that clergy find more job satisfaction in the inner-city ministries than in pleasant suburbia. Sadly, quite a number who have responded to God's call to the ordained ministry – to what is often described as 'full-time service' – rule out any call to a difficult area. We have greatly admired those gifted lay people who have given themselves in service in the tougher areas in which we have worked. They did not need to live there. Some lived outside but were totally involved in the parish. Their friendship with young people who often acted anti-socially in their home, their readiness to pioneer healthy and challenging projects and their work within the community, have been a shining light of love in dark places.

Angels unawares

The use of your home is important. For a Christian couple the home is not to be a castle where the drawbridge is always pulled up. The cheerful home, where visitors are welcomed, meals stretched at the last minute, a bed offered to meet a sudden emergency, and where there are parties and fun – this is a Christian home. Quite often you will 'entertain an angel unawares' (Hebrews 13:2, AV) and some of those you welcome to eat or stay with you will be a lovely blessing to the family.

The Christian home is a valuable place for witness, for sharing Christ and maintaining contact with non-Christian friends. Unlike a church or a hall, the relaxed atmosphere of a home does not seem threatening. Supper parties and lunches express the warmth of Christian hospitality. There is a sense of freedom and ease as we talk around the table, and an opportunity for the sort of come-back that is not possible in a more formal setting. Your home can truly be like Peter's boat, which our Lord stepped into in order to address the crowd. If you are willing, he will bless and use your home to reach people outside his Kingdom.

Saying no

By this point in the chapter there will be a growing response from some: 'That's all very well but what if. . . ?' Yes, indeed. We have painted what seems an ideal picture. That is always the problem with spelling out a principle in any detail. You will not disagree with the basic theme that Christian love reaches outwards as well as upwards and inwards. Holding that always before us we nevertheless have to be very flexible and sensitive to the changing circumstances of home, family, health and talents.

We *do* believe in a drawbridge for the home! The family that cannot pull up the drawbridge from time to time will fragment. An open home policy can sabotage a marriage if it means the draining of resources and energy at all times of day or night. Your love for each other is fundamental to the health of the marriage and family. If you do not have time together, and if the family can hardly ever be alone, you need to hear alarm bells. Then you must decide when and how you will close the door. You must be ready to say, 'Not this evening,' as you are engaged to be at home together. Sadly, if you let them, some people will become leeches, who are round at your home constantly. This will not be good for them or for you. Getting the right balance between opening and closing is never easy. There is a need for constant awareness and adjustment, and not just in the light of the changing needs of your family, but because of the demands made upon both of you.

Another trap to beware of is the 'being out all the time' syndrome. Tragically, we have seen several marriages run into trouble because the Christian partners have felt they must serve, serve, serve. One or the other, or both, go out almost every evening. The husband comes back from work and is out within the hour to a church meeting or activity. The wife, who has had to cope all day at home with the family, is thus denied any real contact with her husband on that day. She may also go out to work and the same thing may happen or both may be out at evening meetings and the children far too frequently left with the baby-sitters or, later, on their own. The saddest remark we heard in this connection came from a wife in a marriage in which both partners had come to faith after they were married. The man became involved in church work in almost every minute of his free time, and his wife said: 'Our love was fine until we became Christians.'

Similarly, there is sharp relevance in the story of the clergy wife who rang for an appointment to talk to her husband, because he always gave priority to everyone but her. In both examples, the call for Christians to give themselves in serving others had been taken to vastly unreasonable lengths. This is only *one* of the loves in a Christian's life. So, even though the people at your church may not understand, and though the pressures to do more may be very persuasive, keep the balance. Know when to say 'yes' and when to say 'no'. Discuss it together. Ensure that your love for God, your love as a couple, your love as a family and your love to others *all* flourish.

The contagion of love

As our children grow up, serving is often *to* them and *through* them to others. If we have welcomed people into the home, they will want to do the same. The warmth, love, joy and fun of your home may be an eye-opener to some of their friends for whom yours may be their first experience of a Christian home. The presence of Christ is communicated even without a specifically Christian word being spoken. It is not always good for the furniture, or for the carpets, but these are things, not people. Again, the balance has to be struck or your children's friends will be around *every* evening – especially if you feed them well!

Thus, a loving marriage creates a home permeated with an atmosphere of love which naturally incorporates service to others. It is a moving experience to see your children 'catching the atmosphere' themselves, and freely initiating or supporting their own caring projects – perhaps sponsoring a child in a Third World country, planting a tree in a barren area of the world, helping in an old people's home or painting an elderly person's living room – as well as taking a lead in the church. They often enlarge our own vision and jolt us out of the rut of service into which we have settled. We thank God for such stimulation from our own family.

Thus, as the wedding service reminds us in its opening exhortation: 'In marriage husband and wife belong to one another, and they begin a new life together in the community.' The two aspects go hand in hand. The prayer follows: '. . .reign in the home of these your servants as Lord and King; give them grace to minister to others as you have ministered to men' (a good reminder of all the love we receive from our Lord). It goes on: 'and grant that by deed and word they may be witnesses of your saving love to those among whom they live.' May your married life and ours be a true Amen to that prayer.

Questions for discussion

Marriage is not intended to be purely selfish but to be a relationship which benefits others as well. Is this the case for you?

1. Read Acts 18:1–4 and 18–28 together. Talk about how Aquila and Priscilla share their lives with others. Do you think these points can be applied to your marriage?
2. Consider your relationship. Do you think that others might view you as exclusive? Do you want to change?
3. List some ideas and ways in which you might serve others together. Discuss whether they are practicable and then make plans to put them into action.

13. Under Strain

The greatest saint gets headaches like everyone else. Strain is inevitable in life. The strain felt by our Lord on the night before he died on the cross caused his sweat to drop like blood in the Garden of Gethsemane. He wept over Jerusalem because it rejected his message.

Paul bore considerable strain as a result of very difficult circumstances (including shipwreck and persecution), as he bore the daily burden of the churches and as his heart ached with love for the people he met. In 2 Corinthians 6 and 7 Paul gives a graphic description of some of the pressures he endured. At one point (chapter 7:5), he speaks of being 'harassed' (under pressure) 'at every turn – conflicts on the outside, fears within'. Strain comes from many causes, but it is our physical frame that always feels the impact. Marriage can be an enormous help when we are under strain as it should be a place of sharing, of talking things over and facing issues together. Sadly, marriage can also itself become a cause of strain.

Gold tested by fire

Before looking at the detail, there is one underlying principle to grasp. It emerges from Paul, who seems to have known more strain than any other apostle. At the start of his second letter to the Corinthians he writes from the heart of 'the God of all comfort who comforts us in all our troubles'. Paul sees God's comfort not just as something to receive and from which to benefit, but as an experience to be used for comforting others. Our pilgrimage is always to be one of learning and training. When, in verses 8–9, he writes of being at the end of his tether – even of being at the point of death – he tells how this experience helped him and his companions: 'But this happened that we might not rely on ourselves but on God, who raises the dead.' Handling strain with God can have a deepening effect on our Christian lives – so that if we do not react adversely we come out of it as gold tested by fire.

It is a rich and valuable benefit of your relationship as husband and wife that you can now face strain together – with God. Many times you will bring these concerns with full hearts to your Lord in prayer. Even when the strain is between you both, the aim must be the same, however difficult it is to achieve it. Persist until you can talk, share and pray.

A fallen world

One of the strains is one you share with all human beings. It comes from living in a fallen world, a world that experiences storm-damage, ecological or environmental disasters, extreme climatic conditions, diseases and epidemics, its people suffering the fragility of life, failure of others in teaching, supplying goods or running transport, dishonesty, theft, crime – and, in some areas, lack of food, heat or water. If these things are not to overwhelm you, you will need to handle them with resourcefulness, action, patience, trust and prayer. You will also be able to help each other to cope and to keep a proper perspective. Christians have to cope with the same problems as non-Christians. It is *how* we cope that should show the difference, how we can have inner peace, even in the centre of the storm.

However, for Christians there is the added strain that Paul felt so deeply, of a world outside Christ, a world so often against Christ, which attacks the Church by words and deeds and misses all that God wants and can do for the humanity he loved even to death.

We feel deeply about the rampant evil in the world. It is hard to bear and we have been more than thankful not only for the strength we have received from one another as we face all this, but that we are part of a loving Christian fellowship where we can share in prayer for this world. We have also been helped by recalling that many Christians have had to handle so much more – from the early martyrs who were thrown to the lions through to the present day martyrs. Compared with their sufferings our experiences of strain are really very small. Whenever possible, lean on the God of all comfort and be instruments of that comfort to others through your lives and your home.

Personal problems

Strain can also come from difficulties that one of you is going through. When work is a burden – perhaps because too much is required, too many decisions have to be made or there is too much responsibility – the support of the other partner is vital.

There may be the prospect and then the reality of redundancy, with its accompanying sense of devaluation and desolation. It is easier to face this with hope and practical action when you face it together.

Strain may come as one partner finds it increasingly difficult to handle life in the home, with a frantic schedule to get the children to school and fit in the multiplicity of other events in their lives, as well as caring for other relatives in the wider family, perhaps mixed in with the frustration of not having much, or any, personal life.

One of you may become physically ill, even with a long illness needing extended treatment or an operation, or you may experience mental illness. Then there are the pressures that come from pregnancy, the change of life and so on.

All this can be faced together even when a ready answer or cure is not to hand. In Ephesians 5 husbands are told to 'love their wives as their own bodies'. Each should love the other in that way. Yet if you are feeling fit and active while your partner is feeling ill, depressed or burdened, it does take great empathy to get into the other's feelings and adjust accordingly. Strain is eased and even lifted in a partnership of true love.

Elderly relatives

The generation gap is a further cause of strain. In a busy life it is natural to feel that you could manage if you did not have to cope at the same time with all the other generations – you may well have parents and even grandparents on both sides of your families, various sisters, brothers, nieces and nephews, as well as your own children. See family love as a privilege, and one for which to give thanks. We can so greatly benefit by the support, the advice and the friendship, as well as from the stored wisdom of years (as long as it is imparted with sensitivity to the younger generation).

Yet there can be strains. Care for elderly relatives is the family's responsibility and how that care happens has to be discussed with the entire family. What is best for you all will vary – a house nearby, a granny flat addition to your home, a flat not too far away with warden care, a retirement or nursing home, or a room in your own house. If care in your own home is the agreed choice, then the elderly person who is loving and wise will need to give you time to be together as a couple and with your children (if they are still with you at home).

The teenage years
Your own children may bring strain in their turbulent teenage years if their attempts to establish a personal identity bring thoughtlessness or provocatively variant standards of behaviour. You will need to talk and support each other as a couple if you are to know how to handle this. You may well wonder whether you can ever be right, however you react! We think of the girl who stayed out later and later beyond the deadline asked for by her parents until one night her mother went to bed instead of sitting up to see her safely home. The girl was in tears the next day – she thought her mother no longer loved her because she had gone to bed! You see the funny side of it later, but at the time it can become a strain! It's easy to say, 'Have patience, pray or even laugh' – all of which is relevant and would alleviate the strain – but the calm voice of reason can hardly be heard in the midst of the ongoing drama.

Avoiding marital strain
Most of all, you need to talk about strain in your partnership as man and wife. This is, of course, the most serious strain of all those we have mentioned so far. We all know that many marriages – too many – run into rough water, and that the relationship can go wrong, or love wither and apparently die. But there is no reason at all why that should be so for you. In marriage relationships, as much as in illness, it is vital to recognise dangerous symptoms and act at once. Prevention at the start by early treatment is far, far more effective than curing the trouble at its height, and lessens the need for lengthy recovery afterwards.

Commitment

From the beginning of your partnership '*think* commitment' to one another. Do not just state it in the wedding service, act it! Those who start their marriage with divorce or separation at the back of their minds as an option or escape route are far less likely to tackle problems if and when they occur. Commitment is 'for better and for worse. . .'. In the security of that commitment many couples have worked through problems and in so doing have found their love renewed and deepened.

Don't ignore problems

Will you promise to be open with one another when you are aware of a problem? That is specially a word to the man. It seems that women are more willing than men to work at a marriage and, in our counselling experience, women are much more ready to seek help from others or to go to marriage counsellors. The male ego does not like to admit it is wrong and so becomes unable to act even when it recognises problems. Sometimes this causes a wife to hold back from seeking help until boiling point is reached. Couples who have come through the troubled waters of their marriage have more often than not been those who have had the openness to accept the difficulties at an early stage and the humility to go together for counselling or advice.

Openness

The lack of complete frankness in marriage is one of the most frequent causes of strain. Frankness takes time to mature, as trust needs to be very deep if *both* partners are to share, hear, understand, respond and help rather than react in negative ways. It may be something in the other's character or life-style that irritates us until it blisters us. Dare we, should we, mention it – gently, of course? Can we receive it? It may be that one of you does not want to talk about your work or its burdens when at home, but the other then feels not only cut out from a large part of your life but also excluded from the sharing and trust of partnership.

Or if the wife is at home all day, the husband may fail to show interest in her day or the burdens she carries, even though she wants to share and to have his support. Often the suggestion that this shows a failure of love would be met by astonishment. This is why you need to aim at openness from the beginning. You will need to communicate with each other – hearing as much as you speak.

Beware of self-pity

Self-pity is a powerful separator. Appreciation and gratitude can be powerful uniters. There is a danger of retreating into ourselves. Moodiness, self-pity and a sense of worthlessness can all result. This is destructive but all too easy: even someone as strong as Elijah could fall into self-pity ('I am the only one left') and want to die (1 Kings 19).

It is not easy to deal with such a mood. God did so slowly and practically with Elijah, but Elijah was still never the same again. A marriage partner finds it difficult to live with such moods, and patience can be stretched to breaking point. When the causes are not physical, they are usually irrational and unworthy of a Christian. Self-pity is selfishness writ large and the very opposite of *agape* or self-giving love. No wonder it destroys. If there are reasons that need discussing, then do so. Usually the moody, self-pitying person needs a good strong dose of the antidote: a long, hard look at the goodness of God, at all the blessings of the marriage and the good things of family life, and perhaps a reminder of the far worse state of millions of others in this world.

Shun infidelity

Another cause of problems is over-attraction to others. Suspicion can easily be fostered by the attractive office secretary or the handsome colleague. You have committed yourselves to each other and to no other. Interest in and appreciation of others are a part of life, but as soon as one finds oneself thinking about sexual attraction, or as soon as one starts making a comparison with one's own spouse (he or she is so good at this and that and the other, he is more handsome, she is more beautiful), your marriage is bruised or even infected.

The ability to see the real person you have married, rather than the outward appearance or talents, is vital. You mature together. You are both in irreversible decay – but as Christians you can be renewed in your spirit every day, and be young and fresh inside the crinkliest skin or under the baldest scalp! The unfaithful man who has run off with a younger woman has often learnt the hard way that he had taken for granted his wife's understanding, care, kindness and love. Now he finds that the new relationship is immature: there has been no growing together. You are to love each other 'till death us do part'.

Reason, don't row

What about blazing arguments? We hear some say: 'If you don't have frequent rows you're not in love.' Do not believe them! We are greatly in love and we have not always agreed, but we have not had blazing rows. Some fiery personalities may feel they have to clear the air with a good row, but we question whether this is necessary. Although there is a right anger over injustice in the world, in marriage the usual reason for anger is your failure to get your own way, possibly further provoked by your mood or physical state. Right may be on your side, but love will share, be open, talk and discuss rather than blaze. There is no justification for outbreaks of anger.

Of course, it may be that one partner tries to tackle a problem without anger, but the other cannot take it and will not admit to being wrong – another form of selfishness – and so initiates an argument in response. Certainly it is better to have a row than to seethe inside with silent fury. Conflict is not to be avoided but resolved. Yet the best way is always discussion, in a spirit of give and take. As Christians, your love for each other should be greater than any disagreement. Your thankfulness for each other, your wanting to please the other, and the joy of being a couple blessed with the privilege of being married, should transform any situation.

Apologise and forgive

'Sorry' is an important word in marriage. British people say 'sorry' very frequently. Our American friends say, as they arrive in Britain, 'We are back in sorry country.' Some of us even say sorry when someone treads on our foot! Yet the word does not come so easily in marriage. As individuals we often hang on to our sense of worth by insisting that we are right. It is always humbling for us to say we are wrong and to apologise. Somehow the very closeness of the marriage partnership makes this more difficult and even

If there is no repentance, forgiveness is not easy.

embarrassing. That may be because we sense that as a couple we should be of one mind (but then we reckon it should be *our* mind with which the other concurs, such is the deviousness of our nature!).

The other side of the coin is the readiness to forgive. If one of you says sorry, then it ought to be possible for the other to forgive, freely and immediately. If there is no repentance, then forgiveness is not so easy – some would say it is not justified – yet often it is possible to forgive because you can discern and understand what caused the word or action and know it to be out of character. The scriptural requirement that Christians should 'Be kind and compassionate to one another, forgiving each other, just as in Christ God forgave you' (Ephesians 4:32) must clearly be even more relevant in the closeness of marriage.

There is, then, one rule that we suggest you establish now and keep always: 'Do not let the sun go down while you are still angry' (Ephesians 4:26). In other words, never, never, never go to sleep at the end of the day without apologising, forgiving and sorting it out. The reason Paul gives is that we must 'not give the devil a foothold'. If the disagreement is allowed to go into the night and into another day it will fester. The balm of love's ointment needs to be applied to prevent that happening, or else the festering becomes a deep sore, a cause of increasing strain and an opening for the devil to get into the situation.

One of the prayers in the wedding service is: 'May their life together witness to your love in this troubled world; may unity overcome division, forgiveness heal injury, and joy triumph over sorrow,' and it adds, 'through Jesus Christ our Lord.' By the grace of Christ make this true in your married life.

Questions for discussion

Strain is unavoidable in marriage – it would be unrealistic to think that this will not be the case for you.

1. List potential or actual pressures that occur in or affect your relationship together. How do you cope with them? Is your partner aware of the things that you consider to be strains and vice versa?
2. Discuss together a pressure or strain you have dealt with in the past. Would there have been easier ways to resolve the situation? Did you relate well and openly or was there room for improvement? In what way?
3. Are there issues in your marriage which are obstructing your growth together? Are there things that you need to apologise for, forgive or sort out? How will you resolve to 'not let the sun go down on your anger'?

14. Sensitivity

Sensitivity is vital in every marriage. Although sensitive people can easily get bruised (as they do not have 'thick skins') and may sometimes interpret a saying or action as hurtful, even though it is entirely neutral, an insensitive person can be like a bull in a china shop or a big-footed rhinoceros, leaving a trail of bruised and broken people! Blatant insensitivity in marriages makes us wince – we are thinking of the sharp, thoughtless and inconsiderate remark to a spouse in public; of the husband who returns home very late without a phone call; of either partner not seeing the other's tiredness, strain or needs. If there is any truth in the saying: 'You only hurt the one you love,' it is usually because you do not expect to be hurt in return. But trying to get rid of your anger or frustration by passing it on to another is cheap and nasty and can be deeply damaging. In a Christian marriage we should never want to hurt the one we love. And this calls for sensitivity.

In the image of God
Sensitivity begins with our regard for one another as people made equally in the image of God. We know the truth, but we do not always carry it through into our attitudes. Time and again we hear wives saying they are devalued, not affirmed in their self-worth and barely appreciated. Is that because deep down men still think they are superior to women? It is said that many men think of themselves in terms of intelligence first and of looks second, but think of women in terms of beauty first and intelligence second.

There is nothing wrong in the appreciation of a woman's beauty – it is the way God has made us. However, if a wife feels that her husband values her primarily because of her looks, she will have an increasing sense of insecurity which will be reinforced every time she sees television advertisements, magazines and articles featuring beautiful women, and she will have great difficulty accepting her advancing years.

It *is* highly derogatory to think of women as less intelligent. In conversation some men pay attention to a comment or question from a man but give little or no serious consideration to a question or comment from a woman.

On the other hand, a man wants to be affirmed as a man. He does not want to feel a wimp or be regarded as such, because his wife makes cutting comments in public. The hen-pecked husband is not merely a figment of the cartoonist's imagination.

In Christian marriage your affirming of one another in your womanhood and manhood should clearly be better than the often warped approaches of the non-Christian world, where using and abusing women as sex symbols or servile partners dishonour the creator's intention.

Affirming a man as a man will require discernment of how he thinks. He may feel that his manhood is fulfilled in sporting prowess, in success at work, in do-it-yourself hobbies or in taking responsibility on outings, and if so, his wife will take pleasure in encouraging him. Wherever possible, she will support the man as a man. He will usually want to pay, to give the restaurant order, and often drive the car. Wives, is that all right with you? He has greater physical strength and so will feel it his role to handle the heavy jobs. Let him do them! The man will feel fulfilled in his manly role. In the joy of sexual union, the man's part is one for the wife to affirm and encourage. Speak to him of his manhood. Enjoy your hunk of man!

Men's attitude towards women is usually in need of a considerable shake-up. Male chauvinism is inexcusable in a Christian. It could be said that it is more in a woman's nature to be sensitive, but even if that is so, the husband has promised to love and that involves sensitivity. The husband may need to make a much more conscious effort than his wife to train himself in sensitivity and must go on working at it through the marriage as circumstances change. It is relatively easy to be sensitive in limited areas of the partnership, rather than letting it permeate the core of your being. Most of all, husbands must correct any tendency to devalue their wives.

As husband and wife you may have different intellectual

capacities or vary in artistic or sporting abilities, but as we have seen, neither partner is of less value because of this. There is an appalling intellectual snobbery in some academic circles and wives often suffer the impact of this. Rating value in terms of intelligence is totally unintelligent! Neither is it sporting to look down on someone who is not good at sport, as if this makes that person less of a human being. The Christian must constantly see through every external feature to the real person. Our value rests essentially in our being equal recipients of the image of God. That is where value must *always* be anchored.

Courtesy

Courtesy is part of sensitivity. Equality between the sexes does not negate either the giving of courtesy or the delight in receiving it. The man who opens the door for a woman, who assists her in being seated at a meal, who practises the 'after you' on entering trains or buses, and who handles heavy loads is showing courtesy. More seriously, his sensitivity to a woman's physical vulnerability to attack in the street or on public transport calls for careful thought and action – picking her up by car, accompanying her to the door, going the 'extra mile' to ensure that everything is all right.

The tradition that the man walks outside when accompanying his wife along the street was presumably started in order to protect her from mud or water splashes from vehicles. It was also a position for quick action with the sword! Some of us retain this courtesy, not because it is necessary, but because it has been, in our generation's upbringing, a mark of respect and care by the husband for his wife. Little things like this matter. Some men always stand when a lady comes into the room. It is overdone if it happens too frequently during a meeting or in a lounge, but it *is* a courteous action. Other traditions may take their place in your generation.

Thoughtfulness

Both partners enjoy appreciation. The noticing of a new hair-do, new dress, new tie, or new shirt means a lot. Failing to notice means a lot too! Thoughtfulness means that you remember to say thank you for a meal, appreciate trouble taken on your behalf, phone frequently if away from your partner, put a note in the suitcase for the other to find, send flowers or a card, and delight in making gifts. We must never take one another for granted, nor cease to take an interest in our partner. This is so much more than the externals, of course. It means being interested in each other's day. It means appreciating the need to share, however tired you may feel. On the other hand, it is a recognition of exhaustion and knowing when time for silence and recovery is the priority.

Misunderstandings

As the years pass you gradually learn to read one another like an open book and can seldom keep something secret. A mood, a word, volubility or silence will all send signals. This can enable constructive criticism or comment, but in the early years of marriage it is in this area that misunderstandings can arise. Just as when you mix with people of another culture you have to get used to their ways and the meaning of their words (such as when an American says, 'Call in and see us,' he means it; when a Briton says it, you would be wise to check!), so it is between you.

In your different upbringings you will have developed different ways of thinking, speaking and acting. You will unconsciously have developed your own body language. There are more innate differences between men and women than most of us realise. So, for instance, if a wife seeks to be sensitive in making a suggestion, the language used may be read by the husband as a command which he resents. A phrase may be seen as helpful by a wife but as critical by a husband. The man may act in what he deems to be a caring way, and the woman may see it as his taking action without consultation. The woman may want to make a decision about something and raises the matter gently. The man, unsure of the most loving response – whether to confirm it or discuss it or suggest alternatives – may respond 'wrongly'. It takes time to learn what each other's language means and, while you are learning, you should not dissolve into tears or go off in a huff over what is often a genuine misunderstanding rather than insensitivity.

'What does this do to my partner?' is a question to ask ourselves frequently. The husband meets some old friends and wants to have them home for a meal. In an expansive moment he issues the invitation. But he should have asked himself: What will this do to my wife? Is it fair? Will she suddenly have to produce more meals, stretch the one in the oven, or go without food herself when she has carefully planned the meal? Will she have to change and do her hair when she would have preferred to remain in more casual clothes? Am I about to ruin a rare evening together to which she has looked forward?

Think!

Equally, a wife may ask friends round for a meal, thinking that it doesn't matter because she is the one who will prepare and cook it. But the husband may have been through a terrible day at work and be longing to get home for peace and quiet and simply to relax with his wife. To find unexpected guests and have to give himself for the evening can be the last straw. It is all made worse if there has been no warning phone call.

Either way, to arrive home with unexpected guests is not fair. It is insensitive in the extreme.

Don't be dull

Never let your marriage get into a rut. It is not very sensitive to stick doggedly to the same unchanging routines, the same old clothes, the usual boring ways of doing things. Introduce special occasions, celebrations, unexpected weekends away and short holidays into your programme.

Remembering each other's birthdays and your wedding anniversary is a must with a capital M! Celebrating at least these three events is a start and an anchor to the year's outings. It does both partners good to dress up and go out together. There is so much to enjoy in this wonderful world. There are new places, new interests and unfolding joys to experience – and these are double joys when you discover them together. When you can, travel together on a business trip; if you can add on a short holiday or an extra night of luxury in a hotel, do take the opportunity.

Life speeds by with great rapidity and as far as possible every year needs to be fresh and delightful. Aim to make each year the best yet. As you get older this process gathers pace, for you have so much you would still like to do or see. We had a wonderful second honeymoon on our silver wedding – and resolved to have one every five years from then on. Now we think it should be every year! We regard holidays as opportunities for new experiences, and not only have we enjoyed new places but have also enjoyed trying out new pursuits. In later years we have both begun to enjoy mountain walking immensely, constantly surprising ourselves with each new expedition. It is such fun being married!

Friends and relatives
Another aspect of refreshment in marriage is a widening circle of friends. Making new friends can often bring an added dimension to your relationship together. Friends will introduce you to new interests and you will learn from the strengths (and weaknesses) of their own relationships.

Some of those friends will be single. Indeed, we hope many single people will be included. Here your sensitivity needs to be to the fore. Can you enable them to enjoy your marriage and its relationship in such a way that it is joyful rather than hurtful? Many of our single friends are delightful and fulfilled people. They have wisely developed interests, hobbies and a way of life that we love to hear about and from which we learn. You will want to affirm them in their singleness and life-style. That they can often help us, be 'aunt' or 'uncle' to our children, or share in some family celebration or outing is good for us all.

You normally have the same relatives for much of your life and often this can mean that you make less effort to keep in touch as the years go by. This is not necessarily through lack of love but because of the separate development of their lives and friendships as well as of your own contacts, interests and involvements as a couple. You may also live geographically a long way apart. Living nearby makes contact easier. We do need to keep alert to this, and in particular to the ageing process of parents. The phone call, note, postcard from holiday are all greatly appreciated, as well as the times of meeting and being together. Remembering family birthdays and sending cards (and perhaps presents) on time requires almost computerised efficiency in some large families, but the discipline is very important. It is how you show your care. Although forgetting is sometimes inevitable, the regular failure is careless and unloving.

Coping with change
You will go through various changes in your life together, not least the coming of a family. Yet there will also be changes in prosperity

Be known as a loving, thoughtful and sensitive couple.

– for better or worse – and perhaps changes of residence as your work takes you to another area of the country or even abroad. There will also be changes of health, age, and so on. These are times calling for particular sensitivity.

For instance, if you move home and the husband is the one 'out at work' he immediately enters a new circle of colleagues, and faces new challenges. The wife, however, can often find it very difficult to be plunged into a totally new area, having to discover practical information about doctors, chemists and shops, and in particular having to experience the much longer process of establishing new friendships. Membership of the local church will give this a real kick-start. It is often a splendid way into the community. But other friendships in the immediate neighbourhood take longer. Just as the wife needs to be specially aware of the strain on her husband of a new workplace, so he has to be sensitive about the wife's settling into the new locality.

Both of you will need to be *very* caring and aware of the problems your children face as they have to settle into new schools, and make new friends. You will need to help them find their young feet in the new area. Family sensitivity is needed in all directions.

A sense of failure by any member of the family needs careful handling. It may be unjustified, as when, for instance, the husband is made redundant at work through the collapse of the company. He did not cause the collapse, but he may well feel that redundancy is a sign of failure. The affirmation of him as a person and of his value as husband and father is vital. Retirement will not usually include any element of failure, but it does mean a vast adjustment, because, as with redundancy, both partners are now at home all day.

The physical changes in a woman's body at the menopause can affect her positively and negatively. So, for that matter, can the amazing changes of likes and dislikes in pregnancy! Surprise must yield to adaptation. Growing old, and coping with illness or failing strength, call for loving care from within the partnership and without, especially from others when there is bereavement and adjustment to living alone. For you, at this stage of your life, this will perhaps apply more to your care for parents or grandparents. Be known as a loving, thoughtful and sensitive couple.

Personal space

As we have seen, allowing each other space within your marriage calls for understanding and encouragement. When the family is young and your opportunities for going out together are limited, there is even more need to encourage some outings alone or with friends, or the development of a hobby, part-time work or an evening class. Recognise the signals showing a need for space as much as you recognise the signals for love and the bodily needs of your partner.

It is good to add new hobbies as you go on in life. Just as your marriage benefited from the sharing of different talents and interests at the beginning, so its freshness is helped by adding new ones both jointly and separately over the years. Finding a latent ability to paint watercolours, or to wind-surf, or to enjoy classical music, or to play an instrument, or to write poetry, or watch birds . . . (there are thousands of variations on the theme) is stimulating. You will *want* this for your partner and will take the practical steps needed to enable it to happen.

One warning about this. Do not allow yourself to show off if your partner is beginning to learn a skill, or develop a talent or hobby in which you are yourself already fairly proficient. Nothing puts a man off persisting in learning as much as his wife showing up his 'L' plates by her performance. Holding back appropriately is the loving way. Indeed, any word, action or look that puts the other (or your children) down is unfair and insensitive, especially in front of other people.

The language of love

The expression, 'Love is. . .' has formed a long series of cartoons. If we had one of our own it would be that one of us peels the oranges while the other opens those little milk or cream cartons. It springs from experience on both counts! It is also one of the small delights of serving the other. Small things can speak volumes – the hug, the kiss, the eye contact in a meeting (or a service), the touch of the arm, the caring act, or the thoughtful word. The more you know each other the more you are able to speak by look or touch. As your oneness matures, you actually begin to think the same thoughts – even at the same moment. T. S. Eliot said: 'Lovers. . . think the same thoughts without need of speech.' They do if they are really sensitive.

Questions for discussion

Sensitivity to one another is essential. How does this work out in your relationship?

1. Do you consider your partner to be sensitive towards you? How does he/she demonstrate this?
2. Think about your husband or wife and then note down ways in which you could be more understanding, bearing in mind the examples described in the chapter. Plan to act on these ideas.
3. Are there areas of your life where you feel your partner needs to be more sensitive? Describe and discuss these together.
4. Review the treats and special times you have had together. Have there been enough of them? Make some plans (including booking time in your diary) really to enjoy one another in the coming weeks and months.

15. A Final Word

You love each other. In and with your Lord, and by his Spirit, your love can grow, deepen, keep fresh and be fun. Keep the model of Christ's self-giving love always before your eyes, knowing that this is the model of true marital love. Then your love will overflow to others. It will effervesce with joy and praise. It will be inspired by worship. It will draw deeply on its heirship of the grace of life. Sensitivity will be a natural hall-mark of its genuineness.

We end by passing on to you the best advice we received about marriage, and have practised gladly ever since: 'Never stop courting!' Go on enjoying being in love, always. Be the greatest lovers in the world!

Readings and Prayers

1. In Engagement

Abraham's servant seeks a wife for Isaac – but is an example to all who seek a partner – he *prays*, several times, 'O Lord, God of my master Abraham, if you will, please grant success to the journey on which I have come' (Genesis 24:42). On finding Rebekah, he says: 'Praise be to the Lord. . .who has not abandoned his kindness and faithfulness to my master' (verse 27).

A delay in the marriage plans? Love under test? Read Genesis 29:20: 'Jacob served seven years to get Rachel, but they seemed like only a few days to him because of his love for her.'

Genesis 1:26–27: 'Then God said, "Let us make man in our image, in our likeness, and let them rule over the fish of the sea and the birds of the air, over the livestock, over all the earth, and over all the creatures that move along the ground." So God created man in his own image, in the image of God he created him; male and female he created them.'

1 John 4:7–12: 'Dear friends, let us love one another, for love comes from God. Everyone who loves has been born of God and knows God. Whoever does not love does not know God, because God is love. This is how God showed his love among us: He sent his one and only Son into the world that we might live through him. This is love: not that we loved God, but that he loved us and sent his Son as an atoning sacrifice for our sins. Dear friends, since God so loved us, we also ought to love one another. No one has ever seen God; but if we love one another, God lives in us and his love is made complete in us.'

Lord, we thank you for bringing us together,
    for the joy and strengthening of our growing friendship,
    for the early seeds of love which have developed into
        the richness of deepening love,
    for the prospect of our partnership in marriage,
    for the future of life and service together,
    and we ask for your gracious blessing on our growing together in our
        engagement, in the name of Jesus Christ. Amen.

Gracious God, as we approach our wedding day
    we come to ask your blessing
        on the day itself
        on the service
        on our relatives and friends gathering with us
        on ourselves as we make our vows in your presence;
    then we ask for your blessing
        on the start of our married life together
        on our joy of discovering each other more fully in total commitment
        on our laying the foundations of a married partnership that will
            honour you
    In the name of our Lord and Saviour, Jesus Christ. Amen.

2. On the Honeymoon

Psalm 115:12–15: 'The LORD remembers us and will bless us: . . . he will bless those who fear the LORD – small and great alike. May the LORD make you increase, both you and your children. May you be blessed by the LORD, the Maker of heaven and earth.'

Song of Songs 2:2–3: 'Like a lily among thorns is my darling among the maidens. Like an apple tree among the trees of the forest is my lover among the young men.'

Song of Songs 2:16: 'My lover is mine and I am his.'

Song of Songs 8:6–7: 'Place me like a seal over your heart, like a seal on your arm; for love is as strong as death, its ardour unyielding as the grave. It burns like blazing fire, like a mighty flame. Many waters cannot quench love; rivers cannot wash it away.'

Matthew 19:4–6: '"Haven't you read," he replied, "that at the beginning the Creator 'made them male and female', and said, 'For this reason a man will leave his father and mother and be united to his wife, and the two will become one flesh'? So they are no longer two, but one. Therefore what God has joined together, let man not separate."'

Ephesians 5:21–33: 'Submit to one another out of reverence for Christ.

'Wives, submit to your husbands as to the Lord. For the husband is the head of the wife as Christ is the head of the church, his body, of which he is the Saviour. Now as the church submits to Christ, so also wives should submit to their husbands in everything.

'Husbands, love your wives, just as Christ loved the church and gave himself up for her to make her holy, cleansing her by the washing with water through the word, and to present her to himself as a radiant church, without stain or wrinkle or any other blemish, but holy and blameless. In this same way, husbands ought to love their wives as their own bodies. He who loves his wife loves himself. After all, no one ever hated his own body, but he feeds and cares for it, just as Christ does the church – for we are members of his body. "For this reason a man will leave his father and mother and be united to his wife, and the two will become one flesh." This is a profound mystery – but I am talking about Christ and the church. However, each one of you also must love his wife as he loves himself, and the wife must respect her husband.'

1 Corinthians 12:31b–13:7: 'And now I will show you the most excellent way.

'If I speak in the tongues of men and of angels, but have not love, I am only a resounding gong or a clanging cymbal. If I have the gift of prophecy and can fathom all mysteries and all knowledge, and if I have a faith that can move mountains, but have not love, I am nothing. If I give all I possess to the poor and surrender my body to the flames, but have not love, I gain nothing.

'Love is patient, love is kind. It does not envy, it does not boast, it is not proud. It is not rude, it is not self-seeking, it is not easily angered, it keeps no record of wrongs. Love does not delight in evil but rejoices with the truth. It always protects, always hopes, always perseveres.'

Father, thank you
for your blessing on our wedding day
for the privilege and joy of being married
for the experience of being truly one
for the anticipation of our life together in this partnership.

We ask for your help
in being open to one another
in the deepening of our mutual trust
in the sensitivity of our understanding
in our desire to please each other
in the adjustments we both need to make.

We pray that we may
deepen constantly in real love
grow spiritually as heirs of grace
establish our standards and guidelines for daily living
discern the priorities for our life together
be outward-looking in friendship and care for others
and serve you in our marriage
to the glory of Jesus Christ our Lord. Amen.

3. In Married Life

Proverbs 3:3: 'Let love and faithfulness never leave you; bind them around your neck, write them on the tablet of your heart.'

Proverbs 3:5–6: 'Trust in the LORD with all your heart and lean not on your own understanding; in all your ways acknowledge him, and he will make your paths straight.'

Ephesians 3:14–19: 'For this reason I kneel before the Father, from whom his whole family in heaven and on earth derives its name. I pray that out of his glorious riches he may strengthen you with power through his Spirit in your inner being, so that Christ may dwell in your hearts through faith. And I pray that you, being rooted and established in love, may have power, together with all the saints, to grasp how wide and long and high and deep is the love of Christ, and to know this love that surpasses knowledge – that you may be filled to the measure of the fullness of God.'

Ephesians 4:29–32: 'Do not let any unwholesome talk come out of your mouths, but only what is helpful for building others up according to their needs, that it may benefit those who listen. And do not grieve the Holy Spirit of God, with whom you were sealed for the day of redemption. Get rid of all bitterness, rage and anger, brawling and slander, along with every form of malice. Be kind and compassionate to one another, forgiving each other, just as in Christ God forgave you.'

Philippians 2:1–4: 'If you have any encouragement from being united with Christ, if any comfort from his love, if any fellowship with the Spirit, if any tenderness and compassion, then make my joy complete by being like-minded, having the same love, being one in spirit and purpose. Do nothing out of selfish ambition or vain conceit, but in humility consider others better than yourselves. Each of you should look not only to your own interests, but also to the interests of others.'

Philippians 4:4–8: 'Rejoice in the Lord always. I will say it again: Rejoice! Let your gentleness be evident to all. The Lord is near. Do not be anxious about anything, but in everything, by prayer and petition, with thanksgiving, present your requests to God. And the peace of God, which transcends all understanding, will guard your hearts and your minds in Christ Jesus. Finally . . . whatever is true, whatever is noble, whatever is right, whatever is pure, whatever is lovely, whatever is admirable – if anything is excellent or praiseworthy – think about such things.'

Hebrews 13:4: 'Marriage should be honoured by all, and the marriage bed kept pure, for God will judge the adulterer and all the sexually immoral.'

Hebrews 13:5: 'Keep your lives free from the love of money and be content with what you have, because God has said, "Never will I leave you; never will I forsake you."'

Loving Father,
  we thank you every day for one another.
Help us, we pray,
  never to fail in the development of our love.
Grant us
  grace to apologise and to forgive when needed
  widening understanding of one another and
    appreciation of each other's talents and character
  awareness of when self-giving love has been replaced by
    self-centredness
  enrichment of our spiritual lives through worship, prayer and your word –
    as well as by our mutual fellowship and encouragement
  sensitivity to the needs in our home life, our work life, our church life,
    our neighbourhood and the world.
Enable us to live as those who know that it is more blessed to give
    than to receive.
Guide us to trust you with all our heart and to acknowledge you
    in all our ways.
So may our marriage mature in the beauty of your love
    and may we grow towards the whole measure of the fullness of Christ.
In his name, we pray. Amen.

---

4. In Pregnancy

Psalm 128:5–6: 'May the LORD bless you from Zion all the days of your life; . . .and may you live to see your children's children.'

Psalm 139:13–16: 'You created my inmost being; you knit me together in my mother's womb. I praise you because I am fearfully and wonderfully made; your works are wonderful, I know that full well. My frame was not hidden from you when I was made in the secret place. When I was woven together in the depths of the earth, your eyes saw my unformed body.'

Gracious Father,
  we thank you for the precious child growing in the womb,
  we praise you for this wonderful creation of a new life,
  we pray for your loving blessing to be upon this, our child,
    for a deep sense of well-being and security,
    for physical and mental growth under your loving hand,
    for spiritual well-being as a child within your covenant love,
  we ask for your support and help in the experiences of pregnancy
    and for your over-ruling hand in the delivery and birth.
  In your creating love. Amen.

5. At the Birth of a Child

Proverbs 17:6: 'Children's children are a crown to the aged, and parents are the pride of their children.'

Proverbs 23:25: 'May your father and mother be glad; may she who gave you birth rejoice!'

Mark 10:13–16: 'People were bringing little children to Jesus to have him touch them, but the disciples rebuked them. When Jesus saw this, he was indignant. He said to them, "Let the little children come to me, and do not hinder them, for the kingdom of God belongs to such as these. I tell you the truth, anyone who will not receive the kingdom of God like a little child will never enter it." And he took the children in his arms, put his hands on them and blessed them.'

Father, from whom every family on earth is named,
  our hearts are overwhelmed
  as we hold this precious child in our arms,
  the gift of your eternal love.

We thank you, with full hearts,
  for entrusting this new life to us,
  this human being, born from our bodies,
  this delight to our souls and cause of our praise to you.

Enfold this little one with your wonderful love, we pray.
From these earliest moments we consecrate our child to you,
  for your guidance and help – and, most of all,
  pray for the knowledge of your saving love to find fruition
    in the years to come.

We pray for this potential adult with eyes of faith and hope
  and while this young life is especially committed to our parenthood,
  we pray that we may be parents of wisdom, love and integrity.

In the name of Jesus, himself born as a baby. Amen.

6. For the Family

Proverbs 1:8–9: 'Listen, my son, to your father's instruction and do not forsake your mother's teaching. They will be a garland to grace your head and a chain to adorn your neck.'

Proverbs 4:1–4: 'Listen, my sons, to a father's instruction; pay attention and gain understanding. I give you sound learning, so do not forsake my teaching. When I was a boy in my father's house, still tender, and an only child of my mother, he taught me and said, "Lay hold of my words with all your heart."'

Mark 9:36–37: 'He took a little child and had him stand among them. Taking him in his arms, he said to them, "Whoever welcomes one of these little children in my name welcomes me; and whoever welcomes me does not welcome me but the one who sent me."'

Ephesians 6:1–4: 'Children, obey your parents in the Lord, for this is right. "Honour your father and mother" – which is the first commandment with a promise – "that it may go well with you and that you may enjoy long life on the earth."
   Fathers, do not exasperate your children; instead, bring them up in the training and instruction of the Lord.'

Gracious Father,
   we thank you with all our hearts for our family,
   we are conscious of the responsibility of bringing up children,
   we pray for insight, discernment and unfailing love in this joyful task.

Grant, we pray,
   that we may be a true example of constant love and care
      in our own partnership,
   that we may help our children to discern right from wrong
      and to be able to stand up for their convictions
         even against peer pressure,
   that we may guide our children to think of others
      and not only of themselves,
   that we may have a family home where there is security, fun and laughter,
   that we may encourage our family in the freedom of your family
      – as your sons and daughters by faith,
   that love for you above all else may be a joyful priority in our whole family.
So we pray for your help in our parenthood and your outpoured blessing
      on our family.
In the name of Jesus our Lord. Amen.